The
Movie Ad Book

The Movie Ad Book

By Malcolm Vance

CONTROL DATA PUBLISHING
Minneapolis, Minnesota
1981

Dedicated to the dolls of my life . . .
Aunt Dolly Hyland and Aunt Dolly Gay.

Special thanks to the following people for their
assistance (listed alphabetically):
Judy Annino, Daniela Brown, David Cohn,
Diane Galarza, Werner Greene, Hal Haskell,
Noreen Kremer, Jim Mann, Sam Price, Tom
Tierney, and my agent, Lewis Chambers.

CONTROL DATA PUBLISHING
a Control Data Company

Library of Congress Cataloging in Publication Data

Vance, Malcolm.
  The movie ad book.

  1. Moving-picture industry—
California—Hollywood—
History. 2. Advertising—Motion pictures. I. Title.
PN1993.5.U65V36   384'.8'0979494   81-9809
ISBN 0-89893-503-2   AACR2
ISBN 0-89893-301-3 (pbk.)

A James R. Mann Production

Contents

Introduction

To some people, movies are art; to others, they are entertainment and reflections of cultural trends. But to the advertising agencies responsible for getting people to pay to see them, they are products. In order to be successful, movies have to sell. And in order to sell, they have to be packaged in a way that will grab the public's attention.

The business of selling movies is a tricky one. Essentially, a movie is a product like any other—a light bulb, for example. But while the marketing of light bulbs has settled down over the years to a more or less happy formula, movies are another matter. Determining exactly what will make a movie attractive has always been something of a mystery. What will catch people's interest? What will make them respond positively—and spend their money?

The creation of a television commercial or a theater preview for a movie usually involves choosing one or more excerpts and then writing advertising copy to go along with it. This type of advertisement may run for as long as a full minute; in other words, the agency can feel reasonably sure that it will have sixty seconds or so in which to promote its product. And people will normally watch a commercial or a preview; they're sitting in front of the screen anyway, and many of them won't run out of the room to avoid an advertisement.

The print medium, on the other hand, requires an entirely different approach. In as few words as possible, using graphics that are as appealing as possible, the agency must entice its "customers" to "buy" a particular movie. Meanwhile, the reader is free to turn the page of the magazine (or newspaper) at any time, and even an exceptional ad may not hold a person's attention for a full minute. So the movie ads have to be very effective very quickly and, more often than not, do its job in a very limited space. It has much to accomplish without giving the plot away; for if it did, who would bother to see the movie?

The success or failure of a movie ad often depends on a single line of copy. This line of copy can be (and frequently is) provocative. For example: "You'll be possessed by the love madness of *Possessed*" or "I was a good girl . . . wasn't I?" That last line had moviegoers dying to know just how bad the female lead in *My Foolish Heart* really was.

Sometimes a winning blurb of copy can be nothing but a simple, nonspecific description—as in "Three Great Stars in M·G·M's Thrilling

True-To-Life Drama" (*Our Vines Have Tender Grapes*). And sometimes ad copy can draw on information the public already has—as in "Gable's Back and Garson's Got Him!" (*Adventure*). Most people, at the time this movie was released, knew that Clark Gable had just been discharged from the army and that this was his first starring role since then; the ad also told them that Greer Garson was his co-star.

There have been other intriguing movie ad lines over the years:

"It's Here! The thundering story that challenges all filmdom to match its excitement!" (*Santa Fe Trail*)

"The greatest adventure a man ever lived . . . with a woman!" (*The African Queen*)

"Once it was human—even as you and I . . . ." (*The Fly*)

"I want to live like a man . . . and still be a woman!" (*Hilda Crane*)

"They're young . . . they're in love . . . and they kill people." (*Bonnie and Clyde*)

"I am Tondelayo!" (*White Cargo*)

"The most astounding motion picture since motion pictures began!" (*House of Wax*)

Notice that the exclamation point is practically *de rigueur*—as are ellipses, those little dots that tell you something has been left out (and make you want to know what).

The visuals of a movie ad—the photograph, an illustration, or a graphic design that accompanies the copy—can also make it or break it. It is generally assumed that the star or stars should be featured. If possible, a star should be depicted "in character;" that is, in the role he or she plays in the film. A glamorous head shot is also acceptable. In the *Stella Dallas* ad, Barbara Stanwyck is shown wearing a negligee and posing insolently with one hand on her hip. In the *Flamingo Road* ad, Joan Crawford is dressed in a cheap, tarty dress and dangles a cigarette between her lips. And the ad for *The Women* featured the film's three principal stars—Norma Shearer, Joan Crawford, and Rosalind Russell—bedecked in the Adrian gowns they wore in the final scene.

Sometimes caricatures of actors and actresses are used, as in the ad for *The Iron Petticoat* starring Bob Hope and Katharine Hepburn. Occasionally the ad agency stretches the truth—or reduces it, as the case may be. The ad for *The Little Foxes* gave Bette Davis a Petty-girl figure that she never possessed, even in her youth.

When putting an ad together, the agency also has to take billing into consideration. All major stars have clauses written into their contracts detailing how and when their names should appear. These apply not only to screen credits but also to print and film advertising as well. In the 1930s, both George Arliss and Paul Muni insisted that their names be preceded by the formal "Mr." Katharine Hepburn has always insisted on top billing, deferring only to Spencer Tracy. Top directors like Alfred Hitchcock, John Ford, Frank Capra, David O. Selznick, and Cecil B. DeMille insisted that their names appear above the titles of their films; this was often justified, since they were as much a draw as the stars. In today's market Francis Ford Coppola, Martin Scorcese, Roman Polanski, Federico Fellini, and Ingmar Bergman still attract the public in this way.

Although the techniques used in creating print ads have not changed much over the decades, the graphics have gradually become more sophisticated. The clutter which typified most ads of the 1930s and 1940s has slowly been replaced by singular, more striking images. During the 1960s and 1970s, "logo" ads—those in which the graphic element is almost a symbol—were introduced, and clever, innovative, gimmicky ads abounded. A prime example of this approach was the advertisement for *The Fox*. At first glance, one sees a line drawing of the heads of two women with flowing hair; on closer examination, the flowing hair becomes a stylized drawing of a fox.

Similarly, the all-purpose ad copy lines popular in the post-war years—lines like "You'll live this romance . . . you'll love its stars!" (*Till We Meet Again*)—have been replaced by more specific, catchier phrases. "Just when you thought it was safe to go back in the water . . ." (*Jaws II*) attracted people in droves, who went to the movie expecting—and hoping—that the water would not be safe.

Regardless of the approach an agency takes, the goal is always the same: tell them anything, but get them into the theater! Werner Greene, vice-president of a national film-advertising house, was once asked how best to reach a potential audience. His reply:

> Impact! That's what an ad has to have. You've got to hit them—the would-be audience—between the eyes, as the saying goes. You have to create an interest in the general public. The movie buffs, the devoted fans of, say, Ingrid Bergman, or Ingmar Bergman, for that matter, will see their latest film, even if all you did was put a four-line statement in the paper. But, for the vast majority, you have to woo them, and it can't be subtle. Of course, it has to be in good taste; we always search for quality in our ads. But it should have an immediate impact!

It doesn't matter, then, whether an ad hits people over the head with a message or seduces them with an appealing come-on—as long as it has the desired effect. An ad that has people lining up around the block to see a movie is good, no matter how bad it really is. And the most graphically pleasing, best written ad in the world isn't worth the paper it's printed on if it doesn't get people to buy the product—that flickering, evasive, occasionally thrilling commodity known as the motion picture.

This is a book about movie ads. It is devoted to the most interesting ads produced during the sound era. It is divided, somewhat arbitrarily, into genres. Some of the ads shown here are classics, as are the enormously successful movies they touted. Others, of course, are not, either because the films themselves bombed or because they had little print exposure. In any case, each ad represents the best the agency could do with what it had.

Science Fiction/Horror

While science fiction and horror films have been Hollywood staples since the very early days, it was in the 1970s that these genres came into their own. In the previous decades, these films were produced primarily as "B" pictures, with low budgets and second-string stars. Today, some of these early efforts are hailed as classics. Universal's original treatment of *Dracula* and *Frankenstein* gave rise to many sequels and imitators, but few are considered artistically as successful, and none have had their amazing durability.

During the 1970s these science fiction and horror films took on a whole new aspect. While still frequently employing unknown, or at least lesser-known actors, these films became major box office attractions. Whereas previously these films were expected to pay their way, usually making a small profit, they suddenly were *the* major money-makers for the studios. The budgets for science fiction films have gotten progressively larger, with an increased emphasis on technical effects and space "hardware." However, pure horror films still remain relatively inexpensive to produce, even as their content has become increasingly more horrific and their effects more and more graphic.

The 1950s was a period of increased awareness of scientific technology and of curiosity regarding the exploration of space. Much of this stemmed from a kind of paranoic concern over whether the U.S. could "beat the Russians" into space, which produced a different kind of paranoia—what will we find when we get there?

Forbidden Planet (1956) was a product of this uncertain time in America. As the ad for the film noted, the action was placed at the beginning of the 23rd century. The locale was a remote planet and the villain was "a menace . . . unseen, unknown, unconquerable." What distinguished the film were its excellent visuals and the introduction of "Robby, the Robot" who, appropriately, was prominently featured in the advertising. The ad, however, was somewhat misleading in the beautiful-damsel-in-distress approach, and ambiguous in its presentation of Robby, who was basically lovable, and certainly not the "unseen menace" referred to in the copy. The movie was quite successful, and gave rise to a spate of imitators, none of which measured up. In a way, *Forbidden Planet* was ahead of its time. Certainly there were other good science fiction thrillers being made during the mid-1950s. However, it was not until the release of *2001: A Space Odyssey* that the wonder and excitement of outer space again received such exciting cinematic treatment.

Invaders from Mars, also made in the 1950s, is an excellent example of another type of sci-fi film—Earth menaced. The ads were typically straightforward, depicting dreaded green monsters in the process of terrifying and creating general mayhem among the American populace. Since there were no major stars in the film, the ad played up the story and the action. As in *Forbidden Planet*, the most prominent figures were an alien being and a beautiful woman, the latter, once again, having fainted in terror while being held in the creature's arms. *Invaders from Mars* enjoyed some success at the time, but did not survive as a major contribution to the genre.

Even less notable is *Hangar 18*, an independent production of the late 1970s which opened widely across the country. It made money, then stole away into the night. Because of the manner in which the film was released, the major advertising push was through "saturation" ads on television; print ads were secondary. The film dealt with the threat of some unknown menace which the U.S. government was supposedly hiding from the American people. The ad featured here and printed in the "trade" papers (*Variety*, etc.), stated the film's plot and then showed several of the action elements, hinting at space gadgetry and decidedly down-to-earth car chases. Once again, no major stars were featured, so the film was sold strictly on the strength of the sci-fi genre.

Some films are advertised in such a way as to direct them into a genre whether they belong there or not. *The Elephant Man* (1980) is a case in point. Critically well-received—even nominated for an Academy Award—the film disappointed many who thought they were paying to see a monster movie. This misconception stemmed directly from the ads that featured the title character in his hooded disguise, worn only when he had to appear in public. He was a timid, miserable, and pathetic being, not at all the menacing, lurking creature which the ad implied. The film succeeded financially, although it is debatable whether it was because of or in spite of the ad campaign.

The same cannot be said of *Black Magic*, a 1949 bomb which did nothing to advance either the fame of Orson Welles or the career of his co-star, Nancy Guild. The ad proclaimed the film to be the "biggest picture in ten years," and promised many scenes of grand adventure. Anyone who took the time to read the small type would have noted that it was, in fact, based on Alexandre Dumas' story about Conte Alessandro Cagliostro, an Italian adventurer who posed as a physician, magician, and alchemist. The public was not fooled, and they stayed away in droves.

Another not-too-successful film which promised more than it delivered, *My Blood Runs Cold* (1965), was promoted through ads that hinted at certain evils regarding reincarnation. This film was aimed at the "youth" audience by prominently featuring its two top stars, Troy Donahue and Joey Heatherton, and the trite come-on about not revealing the ending was thrown in for good measure. It has been suggested—none too

kindly—that instead of the vulture poised on the tombstone, the ad might have more accurately featured a turkey.

Yet another film which went nowhere was Joseph Levine's *Jack the Ripper* (1958). However, its failure should not be blamed on the ad. Graphically speaking, the ad was a huge success, filled with menace and terror. The ad copy was direct and compelling (although one might well wonder how Sir Arthur Conan Doyle and Robert Louis Stevenson fit into a story of Jack the Ripper). Perhaps the absence of a well-known star damaged the film at the box office. Whatever the cause, the movie quickly disappeared from the nation's theaters.

Similarly, the ads for both *The Howling* (1980) and *Maniac* (1981) are graphically very successful. The former promises subhuman horror and terror; the latter assures the viewer of ample mayhem and gore. Both films fit into the genre of horror film that developed in the late 1970s and are distinguished primarily by certain advertising techniques that include startling, even shocking, graphics. The approach here is direct, totally lacking in subtly and apparently very successful. These films and others of the genre have made great sums of money at the box office in spite of their general lack of quality and the absence of any notable performers.

The Omen, a true horror film, dealt with the devil reincarnate and was a phenomenally successful film in 1976. The original ad campaign was subtle yet menacing, featuring a kind of logo made from the title with the devil's symbol of the triple 6s nestled in the "O". The ad included here was printed in *The Hollywood Reporter* and *Variety*. It reminded readers that *The Omen* had made lots of money and asked that Academy members consider nominating Gregory Peck as best actor for his performance in the film. As successful as the film was, it won no awards.

As real life gets more and more bizarre, movies dealing with fantasy become more and more fantastic. Whether they deal with devil cults or with futuristic voyages through space, these films do offer a much needed escape. Of course, not all of these movies succeed with the public, but many of them are so successful financially that they are likely to remain a staple of the movie industry.

AMAZING!

In the year 2200, a space cruiser reaches the remote planet Altair-4 . . . and a fabulous, forbidden world opens up to the earth men.

Here are chartreuse skies, two moons, secret chasms . . . a garden of Eden ruled by a scientist-genius and his golden-haired daughter.

They control a giant robot that can think, speak 187 languages, create uranium or diamonds or a modish evening gown—and wreck an entire city on command.

But there is a menace in this eerie land—unseen, unknown, unconquerable—a power that can shatter the universe. And it brings this adventure of outer space to its fascinating climax . . . !

M·G·M
PRESENTS IN COLOR AND
CINEMASCOPE
(MORE THAN A YEAR IN PRODUCTION!)

FORBIDDEN PLANET

STARRING
**WALTER PIDGEON
ANNE FRANCIS
LESLIE NIELSEN**
WITH **WARREN STEVENS**
AND INTRODUCING
ROBBY, THE ROBOT

SCREEN PLAY BY **CYRIL HUME** • PHOTOGRAPHED IN **EASTMAN COLOR** • DIRECTED BY **FRED McLEOD WILCOX** • PRODUCED BY **NICHOLAS NAYFACK**
Based on a Story by Irving Block and Allen Adler • AN M-G-M PICTURE

PERHAPS IT IS NOT FOR THE LIVING TO KNOW THE TRUTH ABOUT REINCARNATION... THAT, IN FACT, WE HAVE ALL RETURNED FROM THE DEAD TO THE FLESH AND BODIES WE NOW INHABIT— FOR THIS LIFETIME, AT LEAST...

Strange things are happening to Troy Donahue and Joey Heatherton and Barry Sullivan in

"My Blood Runs Cold"

If you give away the ending, may your blood run cold forever!

Also Starring JEANETTE NOLAN · Screenplay by JOHN MANTLEY · Produced and Directed by WILLIAM CONRAD · PANAVISION® · FROM WARNER BROS.

BIGGEST PICTURE IN TEN YEARS!

GREATEST CAVALCADE OF INTRIGUE, SPECTACLE, ADVENTURE AND EXCITEMENT YOU'VE EVER SEEN ON THE SCREEN!

BLACK MAGIC

EDWARD SMALL
presents
'BLACK MAGIC'
STARRING
ORSON WELLES
AND
NANCY GUILD

WITH AKIM TAMIROFF · FRANK LATIMORE
VALENTINE CORTESE · MARGOT GRAHAME
BASED ON ALEXANDRE DUMAS' "CAGLIOSTRO" from "Memoirs of a Physician".
Produced and Directed by GREGORY RATOFF · Screenplay by CHARLES BENNETT
Additional Scenes and Dialogue by Richard, Schayer · Released thru United Artists

This lady of the night has taken her last walk!

The swinging purse . . . the swaying hips . . . the sensuous body against the lamp-post . . . then, the sudden glint of a knife . . . a choked scream . . . fleeing footsteps *and over and over he would repeat his brutal, compulsive act of killing!*

THE MOST DIABOLICAL MURDERER IN ALL THE ANNALS OF CRIME! HE BAFFLED THE GREAT SCOTLAND YARD, THE CELEBRATED ARTHUR CONAN DOYLE AND ROBERT LOUIS STEVENSON . . . *THE FILE* ON *JACK THE RIPPER* HAS *NEVER* CLOSED.

JOSEPH E. LEVINE PRESENTS

JACK THE RIPPER

JOSEPH E. LEVINE presents "JACK THE RIPPER" starring LEE PATTERSON • EDDIE BYRNE • BETTY McDOWALL • EWEN SOLON
Screenplay by JIMMY SANGSTER • From an original story by PETER HAMMOND and COLIN CRAIG • Produced, Directed and Photographed by ROBERT S. BAKER and MONTY BERMAN
A Mid-Century Film Production • A PARAMOUNT PICTURES RELEASE

SOON AT YOUR FAVORITE THEATRE

CONSIDER

GREGORY PECK
FOR
BEST ACTOR

CONSIDER

THE OMEN

The Most Successful
Film of 1976.

TWENTIETH CENTURY-FOX Presents

GREGORY PECK LEE REMICK
THE OMEN

A HARVEY BERNHARD-MACE NEUFELD PRODUCTION

Co-starring DAVID WARNER   BILLIE WHITELAW

Executive Producer MACE NEUFELD   Produced by HARVEY BERNHARD   Directed by RICHARD DONNER

Written by DAVID SELTZER   Music JERRY GOLDSMITH   PANAVISION®   Prints by DELUXE

1977 20TH CENTURY-FOX

On October 25th,
a large metallic object crashed in the Arizona desert.
The government is concealing a UFO and the bodies of
alien astronauts.
Why won't they tell us?

STARRING
Darren McGavin ▪ Robert Vaughn ▪ Gary Collins
Joseph Campanella ▪ James Hampton ▪ Tom Hallick
Pamela Bellwood

I WARNED YOU NOT TO GO OUT TONIGHT

MANIAC

"Maniac" Starring **JOE SPINELL · Caroline Munro**

Associate Producer **John Packard** · Special Make-Up Effects by **Tom Savini** · Music by **Jay Chattaway** · Screenplay by **C.A. Rosenberg** and **Joe Spinell** · Executive Producers **Joe Spinell** and **Judd Hamilton**

Produced by **Andrew Garroni** and **William Lustig** · Directed by **William Lustig**

A Magnum Motion Picture
Copyright © 1980 Maniac Productions · Color by TVC

RECORDED IN
DOLBY STEREO

Distributed by **ANALYSIS FILM CORPORATION**
A NEW FILM DISTRIBUTION COMPANY

WORLD REPRESENTATION: FILMS AROUND THE WORLD INC.

Sound Track Album on Varese Sarabande Records

Drama

The classification "drama" is rather all-encompassing, but there are some films that transcend the narrower categories such as "war film" or "biography." Viewed by millions, these are the films which have endured for decades, screened over and over in "classic" movie houses and on television.

Of the ten movie ads featured in this section, all but two of the movies were based on best-selling novels, and most of the ads include a graphic tie-in with the book. The written stories appealed to a wide audience, and there was certainly some box office advantage to the "recognition factor" of the title.

Based on the life of painter Vincent Van Gogh, *Lust for Life* (1956)—at least according to the ads—was a one-star movie, the star being Kirk Douglas. And although Douglas bore a striking resemblance to the painter, Anthony Quinn won an Oscar for his supporting role in the film. Appropriately—and typically—the ad featured a painting in the style of Van Gogh, that used a decidedly non-Van Goghesque subject. Perhaps the ad agency felt that "lust" needed some kind of graphic depiction. Whatever the reasoning, it was a misleading ad, especially for those who had not read the Irving Stone novel on which the film was based.

An "all-star" cast was featured in *Ship of Fools* (1965), based on Katherine Anne Porter's novel. The movie was produced with much attending publicity and released with great fanfare. The ad featured the eleven principals taken totally out of character and context, gathered at the ship's railing. The title was presented in a very clever, stylized manner. The film was only moderately successful. While many critics admired individual performances, the production was faulted for a general lack of cohesiveness: unlike the ad, there was very little interplay between the characters, and very little chemistry at the box office.

Another shipboard story was a huge success, *The Caine Mutiny* (1954). This movie was based on Herman Wouk's novel of that name and featured a virtually all-male cast. The ad gave special attention to the four principal stars: two young actors, both "introduced" in this film, were nestled below in a clinch—obviously an effort to give some hint of sex appeal. It is interesting to note just how many times the ad repeated the movie's title, and how closely it was tied-in to the best-selling book. Despite the overall quality of the film, it would have been a very tough sell without the built-in audience who had read or at least heard of the book.

Similarly, the ads for *The Man in the Gray Flannel Suit* (1956) relied heavily on an audience who was familiar with Sloan Wilson's widely successful novel. The film did, of course, boast three top stars, with Gregory Peck near the height of his popularity. But the ad did little to convey a sense of the film's story. Anyone unfamiliar with the book would have scarcely guessed that the story revolved around the Madison Avenue advertising business, and one man's efforts to adjust to his new "uniform" following his discharge from the armed services. A "tough sell," the film was nevertheless a huge success.

Another troublesome subject, equally difficult to convey adequately on a one-page print ad, was the ad for *Gentleman's Agreement* (1947). Laura Z. Hobson's best-selling novel had dealt firmly and passionately with anti-Semitism in contemporary America. The ad included here was used after some reviews had been received, but the quotes were totally nonspecific, as was the main selling line: "Now it comes to the screen with nothing left unsaid and no emotion unstirred!" The film succeeded, winning three Academy Awards including best picture of the year, and it did much to advance Gregory Peck's career.

The Great Gatsby, produced in 1949, was a major disappointment, although certainly not on the same scale as the turgid 1974 remake starring Robert Redford. The ads for the earlier version played up its star, Alan Ladd. He was at the apogee of his career, having appeared in a series of successful "tough guy" roles. In fact, the ad included here shows Ladd once again dressed in his characteristic trench coat and hat. It was a characteristic costume for Ladd perhaps, but certainly not for Gatsby. The ad was misleading in that it abandoned, for the most part, the successful novel and relied on the appeal of the star, and on the promise of sexy women in low-cut gowns. The critics were not impressed, and Ladd's fans were disappointed in the softness of the almost actionless film. Recently, there has been a reassessment of *The Great Gatsby*, and the qualities of the movie have been found to outweigh the negative reaction of the early 1950s.

None But the Lonely Heart (1944), a film based on a moderately well-selling novel, also represented a major departure for its principal star. Cary Grant had previously specialized in light romances and comedies, with some occasional forays into adventure. In this film, Grant was remarkably serious in a slice-of-life story about survival in the slums of pre-war London. The ad for the movie was somewhat confusing, however. The copy leaned heavily toward the "tale of love" approach, making it sound as though the film was basically a romance. Graphically the ad was more serious, featuring an unshaven, unsmiling Grant, and showing as one of the three women in his life, a definitely elderly Ethel Barrymore. The movie was well received, but it was years before Grant attempted another characterization so alien to his normal screen persona.

James Dean was truly a phenomenon. He made only three movies, all in the mid-1950s, yet his reputation as a major actor and screen star has endured. That all three movies are viewed as classics is more than coincidental. All contained strong stories, and there is little doubt that it was the talent and charisma of Dean that elevated them, that made them a part of screen history. Of the three, only *Giant*—Dean's final film—is not featured in this collection of ads. *East of Eden* (1954) was filmed first, but it was *Rebel Without a Cause* (1955) that provided a full realization of Dean's characterization of the disaffected, alienated youth of post-war America. The ad for *Eden* featured Dean prominently, referring to him as "a very special new star," but it hedged by employing a very provocative logo of male and female figures partially obscured by a tree. It was left to the viewer to decide whether they were engaged in an act of love or violence—or both. *Rebel* ads were all Dean; he was indeed an "overnight sensation," not to mention the film's major draw at the box office. The movie was a great success and it proved to be the acme of Dean's brief career.

Dark Victory was *not* based on a novel, but it has remained one of *the* classic films of all time. It was made at Warner Bros. in 1939, at the height of that studio's creative power. The star, Bette Davis, had won her second Oscar the previous year for her performance in *Jezebel*. Appropriately, the ad was a tribute to Miss Davis, both in copy and visually. Although she shared space with George Brent, there was no question that Bette Davis was the star—the box office attraction. Audiences knew they could "trust" her as an actress, and that she could best deliver a "story of love so exquisite. . . ."

With the exceptions of *Ship of Fools* and *The Great Gatsby*—neither of which was a success—the ads included in this section all shared a kind of seriousness, a respect for their sources and for their stars. Whether they were selling a performer, as in *Dark Victory* with Bette Davis, or a bestseller association, as with *The Caine Mutiny*, they were done in a straightforward manner, with an attitude of admiration that was in turn conveyed to the moviegoer.

JAMES DEAN

The overnight sensation of 'East of Eden'

A portrayal of surpassing impact -- the story of a teenage kid caught in the undertow of today's juvenile violence...

"REBEL WITHOUT A CAUSE"

WARNER BROS. PRESENT IT IN CINEMASCOPE AND WarnerColor

also starring **NATALIE WOOD** with **SAL MINEO** · JIM BACKUS · ANN DORAN · COREY ALLEN · WILLIAM HOPPER · Screen Play by STEWART STERN

Produced by DAVID WEISBART · Directed by NICHOLAS RAY · Music by Leonard Rosenman

watch, watch, watch for **LIBERACE** IN HIS FIRST STARRING PICTURE 'SINCERELY YOURS'

Vote for Audience Awards at your favorite theatre November 17-27

NOW IT COMES TO THE SCREEN WITH
NOTHING LEFT UNSAID AND NO EMOTION UNSTIRRED!

Most acclaimed motion picture in history!

"BEST IN YEARS!"
Walter Winchell

•

"MOVIE OF THE WEEK!"
Life

•

"PICTURE OF THE MONTH!"
Red Book

•

"PICTURE OF THE MONTH!"
Liberty

•

"PICTURE OF THE MONTH!"
Screenland

Darryl F. Zanuck presents

**GREGORY PECK
DOROTHY McGUIRE
JOHN GARFIELD**

in *Laura Z. Hobson's*

Gentleman's Agreement

20th CENTURY-FOX

with CELESTE HOLM • ANNE REVERE
JUNE HAVOC • ALBERT DEKKER
JANE WYATT • DEAN STOCKWELL
SAM JAFFE

Produced by
DARRYL F. ZANUCK

Screen Play by   Directed by
MOSS HART • ELIA KAZAN

AFLAME WITH GENIUS AND DESIRE, Vincent Van Gogh wished, like other men, to be loved, to be famous. But his genius—his demon—drove him into a life of incredible violence. His search for a wife was frustrated by his own frenzy. People called him a madman. His paintings were laughed at. Today they are priceless—acclaimed as the work of an incomparably great artist. This truly extraordinary motion picture tells the story of his tumultuous life....from the frank and revealing novel,"Lust For Life."

LUST FOR LIFE

From M-G-M in CinemaScope and MetroColor starring **KIRK DOUGLAS** in
co-starring ANTHONY QUINN · JAMES DONALD · PAMELA BROWN with
EVERETT SLOANE · Screen Play by NORMAN CORWIN · Based on the Novel by Irving Stone
Directed by VINCENTE MINNELLI · Produced by JOHN HOUSEMAN · An M-G-M Picture

ON THE HORIZON!

COLUMBIA PICTURES presents A STANLEY KRAMER PRODUCTION

VIVIEN LEIGH · SIMONE SIGNORET · JOSE FERRER · LEE MARVIN · OSKAR WERNER · ELIZABETH ASHLEY
GEORGE SEGAL · JOSE GRECO · MICHAEL DUNN · CHARLES KORVIN and HEINZ RUEHMANN
in a film based on KATHERINE ANNE PORTER'S "SHIP OF FOOLS"

co-starring LILIA SKALA · BARBARA LUNA · CHRISTIANE SCHMIDTMER · ALF KJELLIN · WERNER KLEMPERER
STANLEY ADAMS · JOHN WENGRAF · OLGA FABIAN · GILA GOLAN · SCREENPLAY BY ABBY MANN · MUSIC BY ERNEST GOLD
PRODUCED AND DIRECTED BY STANLEY KRAMER

...from OLUMBIA

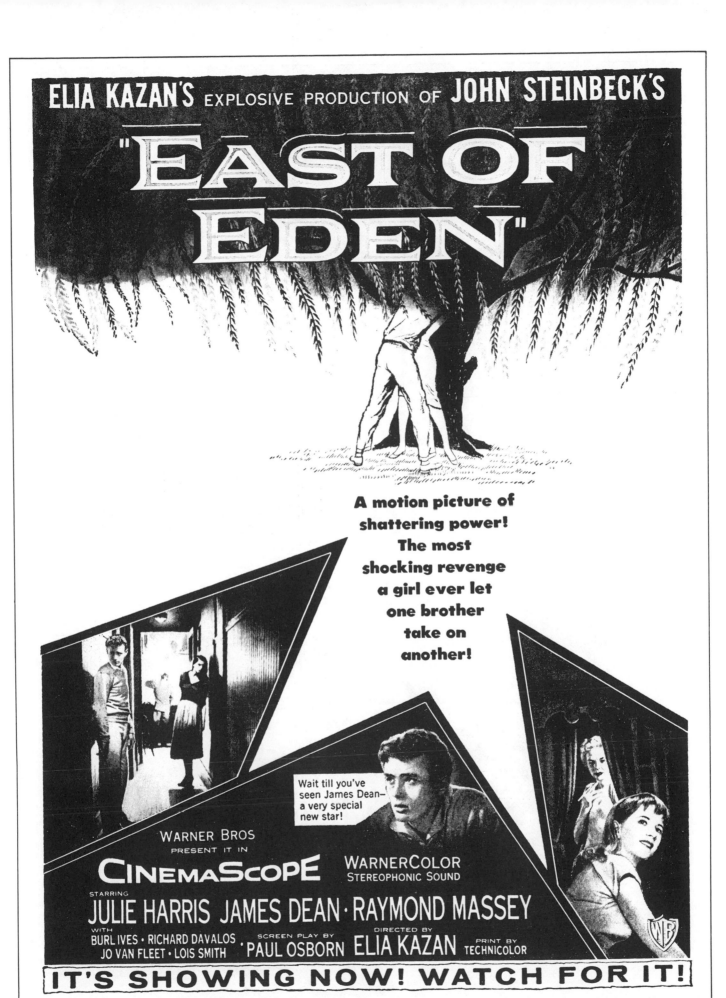

★ **BETTE DAVIS** *Brings You Her Crowning Triumph!*

BETTE DAVIS in 'DARK VICTORY'
GEO. BRENT • HUMPHREY BOGART
Geraldine Fitzgerald • Ronald Reagan
Henry Travers • Cora Witherspoon
Directed by EDMUND GOULDING
Screen Play by Casey Robinson • From the Play
by George Emerson Brewer, Jr. and Bertram
Bloch • Music by Max Steiner • A First National
Picture • Presented by WARNER BROS.

★ **DARK VICTORY** Never a story of love so exquisite!...She smiled at the cost, and bravely paid the reckoning when her heart's happy dancing was ended.

DARRYL F. ZANUCK presents

GREGORY PECK · JENNIFER JONES · FREDRIC MARCH

in 20th Century-Fox's

"The Man in the Gray Flannel Suit"

CINEMASCOPE® co-starring MARISA PAVAN · LEE J. COBB
ANN HARDING · KEENAN WYNN with GENE LOCKHART

Gigi Perreau · Portland Mason · Larry Keating · Arthur O'Connell · Connie Gilchrist
Produced by DARRYL F. ZANUCK · Written for the Screen and Directed by NUNNALLY JOHNSON
COLOR by DE LUXE · In the wonder of High-Fidelity Stereophonic Sound

LADD
Man of Violence and Mystery
...vs.
Women of Wealth and Beauty!

A love story to match the tension of the times.

Paramount presents
ALAN
LADD
BETTY   MACDONALD
FIELD CAREY
RUTH
HUSSEY
BARRY
SULLIVAN
HOWARD
DA SILVA

in F. SCOTT FITZGERALD'S
"The GREAT Gatsby"

with SHELLEY WINTERS • Produced by RICHARD MAIBAUM • Directed by ELLIOTT NUGENT
Screenplay by Cyril Hume and Richard Maibaum • From the novel by F. Scott Fitzgerald and the play by Owen Davis

At last on the screen!

THE CAINE MUTINY

HUMPHREY BOGART
as QUEEG...
the captain and
the cause of
"The Caine
Mutiny."

JOSE FERRER
as GREENWALD...
who understood
the reason for
"The Caine
Mutiny."

VAN JOHNSON
as MARYK...
whose damning
diary sparked
"The Caine
Mutiny"

FRED MacMURRAY
as KEEFER...
the brain
who plotted
"The Caine
Mutiny."

and Introducing
ROBERT FRANCIS · MAY WYNN
Screen Play by STANLEY ROBERTS
Based upon the Pulitzer prize winning novel by HERMAN WOUK
Directed by EDWARD DMYTRYK

COLOR BY
TECHNICOLOR
A COLUMBIA PICTURE
A STANLEY KRAMER PROD.

Mystery/Suspense

From the very early days of sound, films of mystery and suspense were a stock-in-trade of the studios. They were generally inexpensive to produce, and were therefore ground out one after another. Some of them were merely routine, others were downright bad. There were some that were truly outstanding—films of enduring quality, extending far beyond the genre. No matter how the final product was viewed and received by the audience, the ads used to advertise these movies made each sound and appear as though such suspense had never before been projected onto the big screen. In this genre more than any other, the ad copy was frequently used to hint at a plot of startling revelations. Of the films in this genre that survive today, most are notable either for the lasting appeal of its stars, or for the cleverness of its story, or for the particular talents of the director. In rare instances, all three qualities are present.

It is certainly no coincidence that four of the films included in this section are the products of Alfred Hitchcock's genius. He was the master of the mystery/suspense genre—recognized as such at the time, and even more revered today.

Suspicion was released in 1941. It boasted two exciting stars, Cary Grant and Joan Fontaine, and they were prominently featured in the ad. Grant was at the time one of the most popular stars in Hollywood, and Miss Fontaine had just been nominated for an Academy Award for her performance in *Rebecca,* another Hitchcock film (she lost the award for *Rebecca,* but won an Oscar for *Suspicion).* Both stars and the director were top box office draws; together they produced a film of enduring quality, combining the appeal of the performers, the brilliance of the director, and the cleverness of the story.

Strangers on a Train (1951), another Hitchcock masterpiece, featured stars of a lesser magnitude, but one would never have guessed it from the ads. Once again, the director got major billing, but the three principal performers were also prominently featured. The film was excellent, as were the performances—although the careers of the three stars were of relatively short duration. The ad, however, was misleading. The train of the title, while significant as far as plot was concerned, was not a factor in the film's key action scenes—at least not to the extent that the ad implied. But then, would the film have had the same sense of mystery, the same appeal, if it had been titled "Strangers on a Merry-Go-Round?"

The ads for *The Wrong Man* (1957), another Hitchcock film, proclaimed a movie based on "real life," and actually challenged the skeptical reader to check the court records for himself. Very little of the plot was revealed in the ad copy that promised "thrills" and "suspense." The stars, according to the ad, were Henry Fonda, Vera Miles, and New York City. Today the film is viewed as minor Hitchcock, but Hitchcock under any condition is still a cut above anyone else.

Whether *Vertigo* is indeed Alfred Hitchcock's masterpiece is open to debate, but the film remains a masterpiece of the genre. It came at a point in the director's career where there was no need to do more than give the title, a list of the stars, and, of course, prominently feature Hitchcock's name—above the title. Graphically, the ad suggested suspense, a kind of swirling vortex. Perhaps it was best that no attempt was made to explain the plot, which involved a split personality and a fear of heights. Nevertheless, the film—vintage 1958—was one of Hitchcock's most successful, and some twenty years later it was paid the major tribute of being the subject of an affectionate parody in Mel Brooks' film *High Anxiety.*

Whereas Hitchcock's films succeeded despite his work with performers of varying talent (he had a consistent weakness for cool—even icy—blondes), other films of the genre are memorable primarily because of the personality of the star or stars. A case in point is *Dark Passage* (1947), the least memorable of the four films teaming Humphrey Bogart and Lauren Bacall. (The others were *To Have and Have Not* (1944), *The Big Sleep* (1946), and *Key Largo* (1948). The ad campaign relied heavily on the attraction of the stars, whose likenesses were prominently featured. Their names were well above the title, as they should have been.

Another major star in this genre was Alan Ladd, and the print ad for his film *Chicago Deadline* (1949) is testimony to his box office appeal. The ad featured Ladd's name and his likeness; the title was secondary. The insinuation is that the audience knew what to expect when it went to see Ladd in a film. In this case it was a good movie which featured Donna Reed, a rising young starlet at that time.

Dick Powell made a highly successful—albeit somewhat unlikely—transition from the silly-but-wonderful backstage musicals of the 1930s to the hardboiled-detective films typical of the 1940s. Although the ad doesn't mention it, *Murder, My Sweet* (1944) was based on Raymond Chandler's thriller, *Farewell, My Lovely,* which featured the famous fictional detective, Phillip Marlowe. This movie is an example of *film noir,* the French term applied to such films dealing in pessimism and darkness. Powell played the detective and was distinctly featured in the ad. The copy was terse, in apparent homage to Chandler's style. The film was successful, much more than the 1975 Robert Mitchum remake which used the novel's original title.

A later Dick Powell film, *To the Ends of the Earth* (1948), was less successful. Powell was cast as a United States narcotics agent, and was co-starred with the colorful Signe Hasso. The ad for the film promised adventure all around the world, with graphics depicting characters both shady and beautiful.

A classic *film noir, Double Indemnity* (1944) was based on a novel by James M. Cain, and boasted a screenplay by another master of suspense, Raymond Chandler. This ad tells a lot. It features the three principals and arranges them in a triangle which promises devious doings, both romantically and criminally. The title itself refers to the insurance premium collected in cases of accidental death. The unstated implication in the ad is clearly, "but was it accidental?"

The Big Clock (1948) starred Ray Milland, although Charles Laughton, the un-billed Harry Morgan, and especially Elsa Lanchester, were the most memorable characters in the movie. Milland got top billing, and it was his likeness that was headlined in the ad. The story line revolved around a murder and the ensuing manhunt ("the strangest and most savage . . . in history!"), that had a kind of double twist of the hunter being the hunted. Clocks and time were the repeating symbols throughout the movie, but they were not represented in the ad, which instead dealt with the confusion of identification in the manhunt. It is a classic film, shown repeatedly on television and in repertoire film houses.

While there have been a number of mystery and suspense films produced in recent years, most of them have fallen into sub-genres—categories as specific as "a Clint Eastwood film" or "a Charles Bronson movie." The stars have become more important than the story, and with the possible exception of Brian de Palma—and even his films are generally considered "de Palma films"—there is no strong creative force working in this area.

You Would Remember This Picture Always For Its Great **Love Story**

You Would Praise It Solely For Its Thrilling Hitchcock **Suspense**

You Would See It Just To See Its Two Brilliant **Stars....**

And Here Are All Three

OF THESE EXCITING FEATURES COMBINED TO BRING YOU THE MOST THRILLING HOURS YOU HAVE EVER SPENT BEFORE A PICTURE SCREEN

He was charming enough to make many women love him... desperate enough to ruin the life of the one woman he loved.

Screen Play by Samson Raphaelson, Joan Harrison, and Alma Reville
AN RKO RADIO PICTURE

CARY GRANT
Finer Than In "Philadelphia Story" and "Penny Serenade"

JOAN FONTAINE
In Her First Picture Since "Rebecca"

Suspicion

FROM FRANCIS ILES' BRILLIANT NOVEL, "BEFORE THE FACT"
with SIR CEDRIC HARDWICKE • NIGEL BRUCE • DAME MAY WHITTY

Directed By ALFRED HITCHCOCK

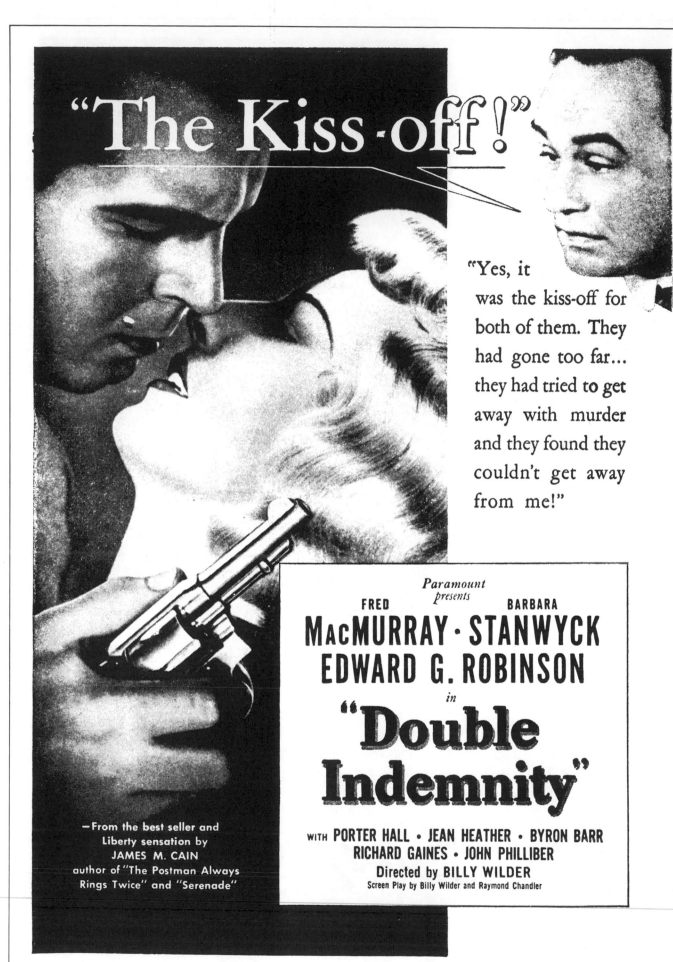

"The Kiss-off!"

"Yes, it was the kiss-off for both of them. They had gone too far... they had tried to get away with murder and they found they couldn't get away from me!"

Paramount
presents

FRED   BARBARA
MacMURRAY · STANWYCK
EDWARD G. ROBINSON
in
"Double Indemnity"

WITH PORTER HALL · JEAN HEATHER · BYRON BARR
RICHARD GAINES · JOHN PHILLIBER
Directed by BILLY WILDER
Screen Play by Billy Wilder and Raymond Chandler

—From the best seller and Liberty sensation by JAMES M. CAIN author of "The Postman Always Rings Twice" and "Serenade"

FORGET THAT FEELING...

She's got MURDER in her heart!

Trouble ahead, mister! That fellow who hired you to find his woman won't stop at murder ...if you don't deliver! Neither will she...if you do!

(Congratulations, Dick Powell. You're terrific in your NEW tough role.)

Dick POWELL

Claire TREVOR · Anne SHIRLEY

'MURDER, MY SWEET'

with

OTTO KRUGER · MIKE MAZURKI
MILES MANDER · DOUGLAS WALTON
DON DOUGLAS

Produced by Adrian Scott
Directed by Edward Dmytryk
Screen play by John Paxton

ANOTHER OF
THE GREAT

RKO RADIO

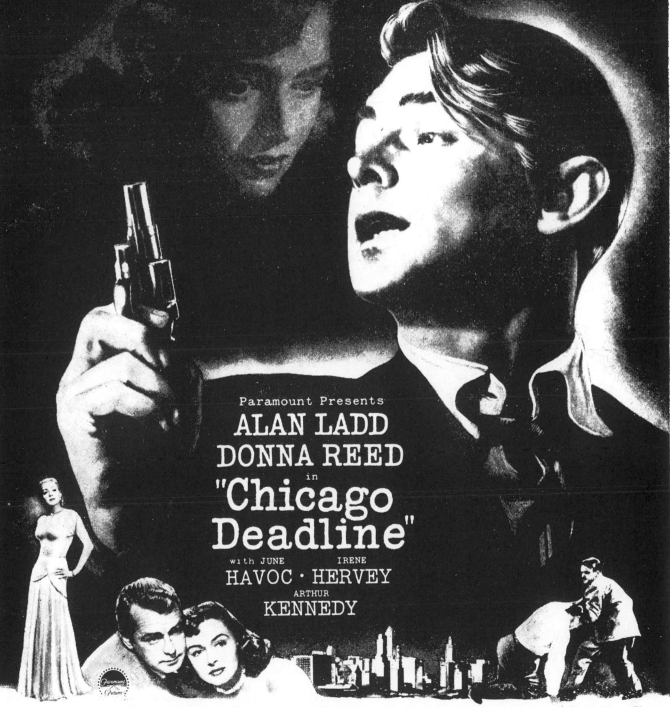

LADD

pays off for a wronged girl who was a 'right guy'!!

Paramount Presents

ALAN LADD
DONNA REED
in
"Chicago
Deadline"

with JUNE   IRENE
HAVOC · HERVEY

ARTHUR
KENNEDY

Produced by ROBERT FELLOWS · Directed by LEWIS ALLEN · Screenplay by Warren Duff · Based on a Story by Tiffany Thayer

WATCH FOR THE WOMAN WITH THE ROSE

in Cairo...
Havana...
Shanghai...
New York!

To the Ends of the Earth

starring

DICK POWELL · SIGNE HASSO

with LUDWIG DONATH · VLADIMIR SOKOLOFF · EDGAR BARRIER

and introducing the Chinese actress **MAYLIA**

Story and screenplay by Jay Richard Kennedy · Directed by ROBERT STEVENSON

A **SIDNEY BUCHMAN** Production · Associate Producer JAY RICHARD KENNEDY

Based on hitherto secret files of the U.S. Treasury and its Bureaus of Narcotics, Customs and Coast Guard. A fabulous story of exotic adventure and romance!

COLUMBIA PICTURES GRATEFULLY ACKNOWLEDGES THE COOPERATION OF THE TREASURY DEPARTMENT AND ITS BUREAUS OF NARCOTICS, CUSTOMS AND COAST GUARD.

THERE WAS A THREAT HE HAD TO DO SOMETHING ABOUT...

There was a threat he had to hide – and a girl he had to seek!...He was the hunted turned hunter – defying the dangers of numberless nights to keep his promise to return!

HUMPHREY

BOGART

and LAUREN

BACALL

From the spectacular
SATURDAY EVENING POST
*serial comes this great
entertainment from*

WARNER
BROS.

DARK PASSAGE

WITH
BRUCE BENNETT · AGNES MOOREHEAD · TOM D'ANDREA

DIRECTED BY
DELMER DAVES

PRODUCED BY
JERRY WALD

Screen Play by Delmer Daves · From the Novel by David Goodis · Music by Franz Waxman

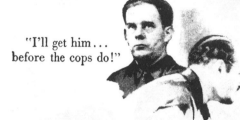

"Alive or dead... I want that man! He knows too much!"

"If he lives...I die...He must be taken!"

"I'll get him... before the cops do!"

"I know who he is...and I'm going to tell!"

The Strangest And Most Savage Manhunt in History!

"All I want is his arms around me!"

"Only I know whether he's guilty...or innocent!"

"Next to his wife... I know him best"

"Nothing on earth can ever make me tell them what I know about him!"

"THE BIG CLOCK"

Most Breath-taking Picture of the Year!

starring
RAY MILLAND
CHARLES LAUGHTON

with **Maureen O'Sullivan** · **George Macready** · **Rita Johnson**
and **Elsa Lanchester** · **Harold Vermilyea** · Produced by **Richard Maibaum** · Directed by **JOHN FARROW**
Screen Play by Jonathan Latimer · Based on the Novel by Kenneth Fearing · A Paramount Picture

For the first time Alfred Hitchcock goes to real life for his thrills! It's all true and all suspense -- the all-'round biggest Hitchcock hit ever to hit the screen! Warner Bros. present **HENRY FONDA, VERA MILES** and the exciting city of New York in ALFRED HITCHCOCK'S

The Wrong Man

Somewhere...
somewhere...
there
must be
the right
man!

STORK CLUB

also starring ANTHONY QUAYLE · Screen Play by Maxwell Anderson and Angus MacPhail
MUSIC BY BERNARD HERRMANN · Directed by ALFRED HITCHCOCK

CHALLENGE! If you don't believe that this weird and unusual story actually happened, see the records of Queens County Court, N.Y., Apr. 21, 1953 Indictment #271/53, "The Balestrero Case"

45

PARAMOUNT PRESENTS

JAMES STEWART
KIM NOVAK
IN ALFRED HITCHCOCK'S
MASTERPIECE

'VERTIGO'

DESIGNED BY SAUL BASS

CO STARRING
BARBARA BEL GEDDES WITH TOM HELMORE HENRY JONES DIRECTED BY ALFRED HITCHCOCK SCREENPLAY BY ALEC COPPEL & SAMUEL TAYLOR TECHNICOLOR®
BASED UPON THE NOVEL D'ENTRE LES MORTS BY PIERRE BOILEAU AND THOMAS NARCEJAC MUSIC BY BERNARD HERRMANN

 VistaVision

Historical/Costume

One of the major fixtures of Hollywood fare has been the film based on classic works of literature, most of them written during the 19th century. As a result, these movies have earned the designation within the industry of being "costumes," although according to the ads which promoted them, they are "historical dramas." The most successful films of this genre are both.

Little Lord Fauntleroy (1936) was produced by David O. Selznick who had a special fondness for bringing literary classics to the screen. He had earlier produced highly successful film versions of *David Copperfield* and *Little Women.* In *Little Lord Fauntleroy,* Selznick presented a character more classic than the story, and it was a tale of enduring popularity. The ad included in this collection featured the two leads—Freddie Bartholomew and Dolores Costello—and a lot of expository text. It was a typical ad approach of the 1930s, and still remains visually pleasing.

Selznick's 1935 version of *Little Women* starred Katherine Hepburn among others, and it was her feisty performance as Jo that gave the film the strength it possessed, elevating it well beyond the level of Louisa May Alcott's treacley novel. Unfortunately, M·G·M's 1949 version got bogged down in the costumes, and June Allyson who, for all her "girl-next-door" appeal, failed to provide enough spice to make this film anything more than a piece of Hollywood fluff. However, it was financially successful, and featured—as the ad ably demonstrates—four very attractive and appealing actresses. They were lovely to look at, as was the film, and no doubt, they had much to do with the film's success.

An entirely different kind of woman was the subject of *Forever Amber,* a 1947 film based on the runaway best seller by Kathleen Windsor. Set in 17th-century England, the book detailed the life and loves of a very successful courtesan. The ad for the film featured Linda Darnell in a very provocative (for 1947) stance, framed by head shots of six of her lovers. The moviemakers were selling two things: (1) the name of a very successful book, and (2) sexual titillation. The movie itself was slow, ponderous, overwhelmed by sets and costumes. It was further restrained by the still-existing codes from doing much more than suggesting the sex which had made the book so successful. As a result, the movie laid a huge egg.

Madame Bovary (1949) was a better film than *Forever Amber,* but was not noticeably more successful. Set in 19th-century France, the story revolved around a woman who had pretensions of grandeur and who created a scandal by her efforts to rise above her social level. Jennifer Jones was prominently featured in the ads for the film, shown in three clinches, each with a different man. Once again, the studio was selling a classic title and the suggestion of sex: "Whatever it is that French women have . . . Madame Bovary had more of it!"

The very title *Tobacco Road* was synonymous with sex. As a notorious best-selling novel by Erskine Caldwell, it had gained an infamous reputation in its portrayal of life among "poor white trash" of the Depression South. Brought to Broadway, it was roasted by the critics—but it proved to be one of the all-time long-running plays. On the screen (1941), even in the hands of a master like John Ford, it was not a critical success, but the public didn't care; they simply wanted to see it. The ads eschewed any mention of Caldwell or his book, but the one line that was used said it all: "At last it's on the screen!" Certainly the film was not a historical drama at the time, but today it is a fascinating slice of the underbelly life of an extremely turbulent time.

Turbulence was the essence of *War and Peace* (1956). The story told the struggle of the Russians against the invading French armies of Napoleon. It dealt with families uprooted, with lives destroyed, with love unrealized. The movie as directed by King Vidor was not the Tolstoy novel, but it was stirring, even great, cinema. The movie was a success—generally with the critics and certainly with the movie-going public. As a film based on a classic novel, it struck an interesting balance—it had a reserved, "classic" quality, yet there were exciting performances by exciting stars who assured box office appeal. There were lots of action sequences, and there was even more romance. The ads featured all these elements—the stars were prominently placed against a background of turmoil, with the book outlined against the whole montage. Truly representative, it was an ad faithful to the spirit of the film.

Another Tolstoy novel, *Anna Karenina,* was returned to the screen in 1947, but this one was not as successful as the 1935 Greta Garbo version. Vivien Leigh played the title role, this time under the direction of Alexander Korda. Despite their combined talents—and the support of the fine actor Ralph Richardson—the film remained rather static. In a way, the print ad reflected this state: there was a quote featured—beautiful to read, but ambiguous and passionless; the book was given a prominent position, as was the likeness of Vivien Leigh. Neither was sufficient box office lure. The ad was too nonspecific, too reverential in its approach—it and the film did not work.

Jane Eyre (1944) did work. The ad promised passion and romance. The key line, perhaps excessive—"A Love Story Every Woman Would Die a Thousand Deaths to Live!"—was very effec-
tive. The two stars were perfectly cast and prominently featured. The movie was remarkably faithful to the mood of Charlotte Bronte's novel and was a huge success. Perhaps the clinch—and Miss Fontaine's cleavage—featured in the ad was a bit misleading, but it really didn't matter; in all other respects, the film delivered.

Passion and stirring romance were not the essence of *Pride and Prejudice* (1940), and appropriately, the ad gave one an impression of lightness and humor. The movie was based on Jane Austen's famous novel, written and set in the 1800s. It was a comedy of manners, the story of a spinster sister who spurns all efforts of her family to marry her off. The ad featured the smiling faces of the two principal stars, Greer Garson and Laurence Olivier. While Jane Austen was not mentioned by name, her book was prominently displayed. Here was a proper and restrained ad that befitted the film.

The ad for *Anna and the King of Siam* (1946) was somewhat less satisfactory. The book had been a huge success, and was based on the memoirs of the Anna of the title. This film, too, was a success, but the ad did nothing more than identify the book as being the basis of the film story. Had one not read the book it might well have been assumed that the movie was about burning pretty women at the stake. The ad had no suggestion of the strange, unrealized love that developed between the two title characters, or of the warmth and charm of the story. But then, so many people had read the book that perhaps the ads didn't matter.

Hollywood no longer produces many costume pictures. Given the sophistication of the average moviegoer today, it would be too expensive to recreate certain historical periods. The financial risk is too great, and movie-going public too fickle. It has been largely left to television, with its huge one-shot audience, to attempt productions such as *Shogun,* while Hollywood concentrates on the smaller, more personal film.

A SON...

PROUD OF HIS MOTHER

... worshipping the ground she walked on ... loving her with a fierce loyalty ... yet at the same time stealing his way into the flinty heart of a proud, tyrannical nobleman and teaching him the meaning of kindness.

Freddie Bartholomew breathes life into Frances Hodgson Burnett's beloved character, "Little Lord Fauntleroy" and gives a perform-ance in the world-famous story that will indelibly stamp itself upon your heart. Dolores Costello Barry-more as "Dearest" his mother, re-turns to the screen lovelier and more radiant than ever. She will delight the millions of fans who have been eagerly awaiting her return.

We'd like to be modest in our statements about this picture — but the facts speak for themselves ... It has a magnificent cast — a perfect story — was directed by John Crom-well who thrilled you with "Of Human Bondage" — produced by David O. Selznick who gave you "David Copperfield" and the screen-play was written by Hugh Walpole, noted English author.

It is a picture that is marked for major screen honors in 1936!

Selznick International Pictures, Inc., *Presents*

LITTLE LORD FAUNTLEROY

with

FREDDIE BARTHOLOMEW *and* DOLORES COSTELLO BARRYMORE

Mickey Rooney • C. Aubrey Smith • Guy Kibbee • Henry Stephenson
E. E. Clive • Una O'Connor • Jackie Searl • Ivan Simpson • Jessie Ralph
PRODUCED BY DAVID O. SELZNICK Released thru UNITED ARTISTS

Whatever it is that French women have... Madame Bovary had more of it!

M-G-M presents

JENNIFER JONES
VAN HEFLIN
LOUIS JOURDAN

Madame Bovary

with CHRISTOPHER KENT • GENE LOCKHART • FRANK ALLENBY • GLADYS COOPER

and JAMES MASON *Portraying* GUSTAVE FLAUBERT, THE AUTHOR

The Madame Bovary Waltz
and Themes From "Madame Bovary"
available on M-G-M Records

Screen Play by ROBERT ARDREY • Based on the Novel by GUSTAVE FLAUBERT
Directed by VINCENTE MINNELLI • Produced by PANDRO S. BERMAN
A METRO-GOLDWYN-MAYER PICTURE

PARAMOUNT PRESENTS

AUDREY HEPBURN
HENRY FONDA
MEL FERRER

in

VISTAVISION
MOTION PICTURE HIGH FIDELITY

A PONTI-DeLAURENTIIS PRODUCTION
Co-starring

VITTORIO GASSMAN

HERBERT LOM · OSCAR HOMOLKA · ANITA EKBERG

HELMUT DANTINE · BARRY JONES · ANNA MARIA FERRERO · MILLY VITALE · JEREMY BRETT and

JOHN MILLS
Produced by DINO DeLAURENTIIS · Directed by KING VIDOR
Based on the novel "War And Peace" by LEO TOLSTOY
Color by TECHNICOLOR

One of M·G·M's Gala Silver Anniversary hits!

Everybody loves *Little Women* ...and they love the boy-next-door!

M-G-M presents its newest TECHNICOLOR Production

Little Women

STARRING

JUNE ALLYSON · PETER LAWFORD
MARGARET O'BRIEN
ELIZABETH TAYLOR · JANET LEIGH
ROSSANO BRAZZI · MARY ASTOR
LUCILE WATSON · SIR C. AUBREY SMITH
HARRY DAVENPORT

A MERVYN LeROY PRODUCTION

Color by TECHNICOLOR

Screen Play by ANDREW SOLT, SARAH Y. MASON and VICTOR HEERMAN
From the Novel by LOUISA MAY ALCOTT
Produced and Directed by MERVYN LeROY

A METRO-GOLDWYN-MAYER PICTURE

FROM the top of every best-seller list it comes...to top all screen entertainment with its warmth and splendor!

Darryl F. Zanuck
presents

IRENE DUNNE
REX HARRISON
LINDA DARNELL

IN

ANNA and the KING of SIAM

with

LEE J. COBB · GALE SONDERGAARD · MIKHAIL RASUMNY · DENNIS HOEY
TITO RENALDO · RICHARD LYON · Directed by JOHN CROMWELL · Produced by LOUIS D. LIGHTON
Screen Play by Talbot Jennings and Sally Benson · Based upon the Biography by Margaret Landon

20th
CENTURY-FOX

At last it's on the screen!

Tobacco Road

with

CHARLEY GRAPEWIN · MARJORIE RAMBEAU
GENE TIERNEY · WILLIAM TRACY and Dana
Andrews · Slim Summerville · Ward Bond
Grant Mitchell · Zeffie Tilbury · Screen Play by
Nunnally Johnson · Directed by JOHN FORD
Produced by DARRYL F. ZANUCK
A 20th Century-Fox Picture

5

Adventure

Of all the various genres of movie ads created by Hollywood's publicity and promotion departments, perhaps the most uniformly successful were those which celebrated the adventure movies. Ads for these pictures seldom used stars as the main selling point. Of course, the performers were featured in the ads, but the main points were the story and the action. These ads were direct, generally succinct, relying on graphics to convey the strong sense of action and excitement that have made these films among the most enduring.

Of the ads featured here, *Two Years Before the Mast* (1946) relied very heavily on pictorials to convey a sense of adventure. The copy merely identified the film as being based on the "Immortal Classic of the Seven Seas!" The pictures in the ad did the rest. They showed raging seas; grim, stern faces, treachery and danger; pain and solace. It was a most effective ad, and a successful movie.

Captains Courageous (1937), another sea adventure, projected more warmth through its promotional ads. There was more copy than with *Two Years Before the Mast,* and the graphics here were more concerned with selling the film's stars than with depicting scenes of turmoil and derring-do. Whereas Alan Ladd, the star of *Mast,* was unquestionably a box office draw, he was not regarded as being of the same magnitude as the combination of four of M-G-M's most dependable—Spencer Tracy, Melvyn Douglas, Lionel Barrymore, and Freddy Bartholemew. *Captains Courageous* was a cut above the standard action film, and the ads were meant to make sure everyone understood that.

As a film, *Moby Dick* (1956) was also essentially a sea adventure; as a book, however, it is far more complicated, and, in fact, the element of true adventure is negligible. The ads, of course, seemed to want it both ways: everyone should know that this movie was based on a classic novel, yet no one should think that the film was lacking in excitement. The most confusing aspect of the ad is the line, "This is Gregory Peck as the fiery man-without-a-woman." It is unclear just what this line is intended to imply or why it might entice anyone to see the movie (unless you conclude that having a randy sea captain makes for a more exciting voyage). Nevertheless, a lot of people *did* see the movie, even though it was not a major critical or commercial success. Like the ad, the film suffered from ambiguity and no real sense of direction.

Treasure Island (1934) was definitely selling a classic tale of adventure. Robert Louis Stevenson's novel had been read by millions of people, most of them while they were still children. The ad relied heavily on association with the book, featuring the author's likeness even more prominently than those of the two ever-so-lovable stars, Wallace Beery and Jackie Cooper. The movie was made to appeal to people of all ages, but the main thrust was toward the younger audience, especially in the cartoon-like characters spilling out of the book.

A classic tale in the truest sense, *Ulysses* (1967) was an amalgam of fantasy and savage adventure. The movie was faithful to the classic Greek tale in terms of action, but not completely so with the principal characters. Kirk Douglas was . . . well, Kirk Douglas; Silvano Mangano was Italian and beautiful. The ad conveyed all these things. It proclaimed the film to be "The Greatest Romantic Adventure of All Time!"; it depicted Kirk Douglas and a tall, exotic, beautiful woman

(Miss Mangano); it displayed a montage of adventure straight from Greek mythology. In short, it touched all bases—and it worked.

Spartacus, released in 1960, was set in ancient Rome. While the film certainly contained elements of adventure, it, in fact was much more than an adventure film. Directed by Stanley Kubrick, the movie was a study of characters, a picture of a corrupt civilization which the ad reflected. Graphically the ad was undistinguished, but it was faithful to the film. The major question after reading the ad, however, is "who is 'her' "? An additional query might be: "What is this movie about?" Nevertheless, it was popular in the 1960s, and—perhaps on the strength of Kubrick's later films—remains today as a favorite in repertoire houses.

The ad for *The Adventures of Robin Hood*—originally released in 1938—was prepared for a reissue of the film, so the copy assumes a total familiarity with the movie and its subject. Graphically it is most effective, depicting a handsome, young Errol Flynn and the always-beautiful Olivia de Havilland. The stars are shown variously in scenes of action and romance. The story of Robin Hood is classic adventure, and so is the film.

Gunga Din (1939) is another classic adventure film, one which has gained in popularity over the decades. Based rather loosely on a poem by Rudyard Kipling, the movie was set in India at a time when the native people were in rebellion against British colonialism. The ad was more or less faithful to the story, depicting soldiers, battle scenes, and general chaos. However, the central figures would imply that romance had a paramount place in the story, when, in fact, what love interest there was in the film seemed to have been thrown in as a kind of relief factor—a pause between battle scenes.

Suggestions that women and/or romance figured prominently in the story of *The Treasure of the Sierra Madre* (1948) abounded in the ad for that film. The copy alluded to it (. . . "And the more they yearn for their women's arms . . .") and the visuals show a woman wearing a low-cut blouse, a short skirt, and a "come-hither" smile. The film was, in fact, unrelentingly unromantic, almost womanless. Except for one brief scene in a town (in which actress Ann Sheridan appeared in a cameo spot "for the hell of it" she said), all of the action took place in the deserts and mountains of the Sierra Madre range. What the ad did convey accurately was the sense of obsessive desperation that possessed the character portrayed by Humphrey Bogart.

Of course, women can easily have a legitimate place in a story of high adventure. *Only Angels Have Wings,* a 1939 Howard Hawks production, was a true adventure film with a strong romantic angle. It dealt with transporting the mail by air in South America in the early 1930s. In this case, unlike most adventure films, the story was secondary in importance (in terms of ticket sales) to the pairing of two very popular stars, Cary Grant and Jean Arthur. The movie was a great success, so obviously the different elements were well mixed.

Virtually *all* of the James Bond films have been very successful at the box office. Since the series was launched in 1962 with *Dr. No,* there have been a total of twelve Bond movies, *For Your Eyes Only* (1981), being the most recent. The ad for this film is typical of the series, picturing James Bond, played by Roger Moore, in action, viewed through the very attractive legs of a woman who is holding a spear gun. The elements common to all these movies have been (1) Bond himself, (2) his gun, (3) an array of beautiful women, (4) lots of gimmickry, and (5) exotic locations—*For Your Eyes Only* is certainly no exception. In fact, the plot is little more than a travelogue, interrupted occasionally by attempts to get something out of the ocean and keep it away from the bad guys. As escapist fare, it was great fun and pleased loyal Bond fans.

The box office smash for 1981 was *Raiders of the Lost Ark*, perhaps the ultimate adventure film. As created by George Lucas (the mastermind of *Star Wars*) and Stephen Speilberg (the creator of *Close Encounter of the Third Kind*), *Raiders* is a compendium of all the cliff-hanging adventures which have been the hallmark of the old Saturday afternoon serials. The ad included here features the rugged hero played by Harrison Ford, and gives a sense of some of the action, although it would take a gatefold spread to depict all the various elements that makes this movie so exciting and successful. *Raiders* is an example of a film which—introduced with extensive publicity and fanfare—succeeded primarily because of word-of-mouth from people who saw it, loved it, and told their friends.

Adventure films of all varieties continue to be popular with the Hollywood studios. These are action films which rely on the thrills and excitement of the visuals to attract the audience—the stars and the feasibility of the story are secondary.

THE NEARER THEY GET TO THEIR TREASURE
THE FARTHER THEY GET FROM THE LAW!

...And the more they yearn for their women's arms, the fiercer is their lust for the gold that must be torn from those dangerous hills!

THE TREASURE OF THE SIERRA MADRE

WARNER BROS. hit a new high in high adventure... bringing another great best-seller to the screen!

STARRING HUMPHREY
BOGART
AND WALTER
HUSTON
TIM HOLT · BRUCE BENNETT
DIRECTED BY   PRODUCED BY
JOHN HUSTON · HENRY BLANKE
SCREEN PLAY BY JOHN HUSTON · BASED ON THE NOVEL BY B. TRAVEN · MUSIC BY MAX STEINER

ROMANCE AS GLORIOUS AS THE TOWERING ANDES!

A continent its stage...and the millions who have ever loved...its audience! It's 1939's greatest screen adventure... with the grand stars of "Gunga Din" and "You Can't Take It With You".

Together For The First Time!

CARY GRANT JEAN ARTHUR

Only Angels Have Wings

THOMAS MITCHELL · RITA HAYWORTH · RICHARD BARTHELMESS

Screen Play by Jules Furthman · A **HOWARD HAWKS** PRODUCTION · A Columbia Picture

Ask Your Theatre When!

This is
GREGORY PECK
as the fiery
man-without-a-woman

This is the
motion picture
so crowded
with exciting
achievements
that it is
impossible to
list them all!
Gregory Peck's
mighty
portrayal
is certainly
one of them.

Co-starred
with him are
**RICHARD
BASEHART**
as the young,
romantic
rover and
LEO GENN
as the
vengeful
Starbuck

In a year of
so many
wonderful
screen
advances
the mightiest
leap forward
of all is
WARNER BROS'.
presentation
of the
**JOHN
HUSTON**
production of
Herman Melville's

MOBY DICK

and
**ORSON
WELLES**
as Father Mapple

COLOR BY **TECHNICOLOR**

SCREEN PLAY BY
RAY BRADBURY AND JOHN HUSTON

WB

A MOULIN PICTURE · DIRECTED BY JOHN HUSTON · PRESENTED BY WARNER BROS.

If Robert Louis Stevenson had traded his pen for a camera...

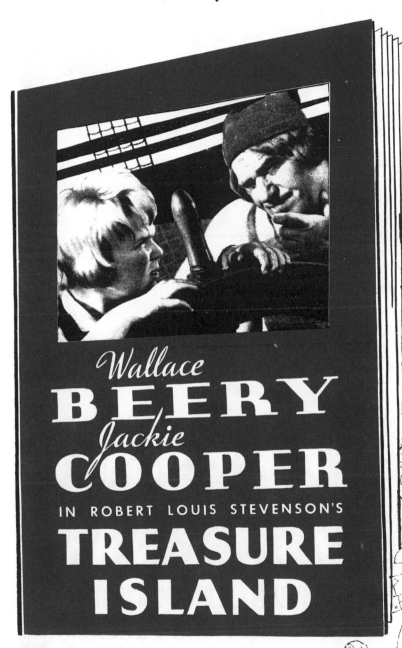

Wallace **BEERY** *Jackie* **COOPER**

IN ROBERT LOUIS STEVENSON'S

TREASURE ISLAND

Little did he know that one day his immortal story of "Treasure Island" would come to life...just as his other thrill-novel "Dr. Jekyll and Mr. Hyde" captivated the world. Two million copies of "Treasure Island" have quickened the heart-beat of men, women and children.

Glorious news that each exciting moment has been recaptured to stir your soul! Wallace Beery is Long John Silver, and Jackie Cooper is the adventurous youth Jim Hawkins, whose boyish loyalty will grip your emotions, as he did before when he adored his "Champ" with tear-dimmed eyes. Lionel Barrymore too, gives his most thrilling performance. See the cast of all-stars!

It is a great picture and Metro-Goldwyn-Mayer is proud to have devoted its vast resources to the production of this, the year's important entertainment!

WALLACE BEERY *as Long John Silver*
JACKIE COOPER · *as Jim Hawkins*
LIONEL BARRYMORE *as Billy Bones*
OTTO KRUGER - - - - - *as Dr. Livesey*
LEWIS STONE - - - - *as Captain Smollett*
"CHIC" SALE - - - - - - *as Ben Gunn*
WILLIAM V. MONG - - - *as Old Pew*
DOROTHY PETERSON - - *as Mrs. Hawkins*
Directed by Victor Fleming • Produced by Hunt Stromberg
A METRO-GOLDWYN-MAYER PICTURE

MAGNIFICENT HUMAN DRAMA OF A LOVE SO STRONG IT SPARKED THE REVOLT THAT SHOOK THE WORLD!

The General desired her... even more than he wanted to possess Rome!

Spartacus loved her!

The Senator stole her...and used her for a cunning revenge!

The Slaver sold her...for a handful of gold and betrayed an Empire!

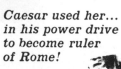

The Rebel worshipped her... as fiercely as his dream of freedom!

Caesar used her... in his power drive to become ruler of Rome!

KIRK DOUGLAS ☆ LAURENCE OLIVIER ☆ JEAN SIMMONS
CHARLES LAUGHTON ☆ PETER USTINOV ☆ JOHN GAVIN

"A MIGHTY TALE TOLD LARGE!" –LIFE

"ABSORBING, COMPASSIONATE!" –LOOK

SPARTACUS

and TONY CURTIS as Antoninus

TECHNICOLOR® SUPER TECHNIRAMA 70® LENSES BY PANAVISION

Directed by STANLEY KUBRICK · Screenplay by DALTON TRUMBO · Based on a novel by HOWARD FAST · Produced by EDWARD LEWIS

Executive Producer KIRK DOUGLAS · Music composed and conducted by ALEX NORTH · A Bryna Production · A Universal-International Release

THE YEAR'S BIG SHOW IS READY! Watch your newspapers for local play-date.

1939 BRINGS THE PICTURE THAT TOOK ALL OF 1938 TO MAKE *!!!*

Now it's yours! . . . Thrills for a thousand movies plundered for one mighty show! . . .

Armies and elephants . . . Love and Laughter . . . . Breathless adventure inspired by Kipling's heroic lines of loyalty and daring! . . . Astride its eye-staggering scenes, three lusty sons of the sword . . . reckless in love, ruthless in war, dauntless in peril. . . . The throbbing heart of turbulent India seething with revolt —and a woman gambling her happiness—as battalions march at dawn!

GUNGA DIN

STARRING

CARY GRANT · VICTOR McLAGLEN
AND
DOUGLAS FAIRBANKS, Jr.

with SAM JAFFE · EDUARDO CIANNELLI · JOAN FONTAINE

Screen play by Joel Sayre & Fred Guiol · From a story by Ben Hecht & Charles MacArthur
Inspired by Rudyard Kipling's Poem

RKO RADIO PICTURE
Pandro S. Berman, in Charge of Production · Produced and **Directed by George Stevens**

ONE OF THE GREAT PICTURES OF ALL TIME!

Freddie BARTHOLOMEW
as Harvey—pampered by luxury
...the sea made him a man

Spencer TRACY
as Manuel—hardy sailor who
taught Harvey the ropes...

Captains Courageous

THE MOST EXCITING PICTURE
SINCE "MUTINY ON THE BOUNTY"

Again—as in the stirring "Mutiny"—
you *live* the roaring drama of men against
the sea. You share the struggles, the heart-
aches, the laughter of courageous souls
who leave the women they love to dare the
wrath of the angry waves...men in conflict with their destiny enacting the most
thrilling story the screen could offer. A
brilliant triumph that takes rank with the
greatest pictures M-G-M has given you!

Lionel BARRYMORE
as Captain Disko, whose life was
lived where men are fearless...

Melvyn DOUGLAS
as Harvey's father whose wealth
couldn't buy his boy's love.

A Metro-
Goldwyn-Mayer
Picture Directed by
VICTOR FLEMING

Captains Courageous
RUDYARD KIPLING'S
greatest story of struggle,
adventure and life!

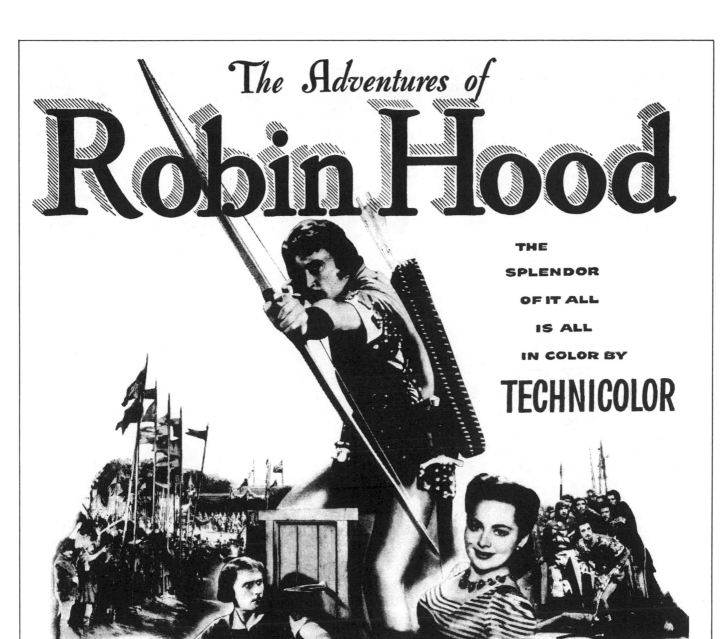

The Adventures of Robin Hood

THE SPLENDOR OF IT ALL IS ALL IN COLOR BY

TECHNICOLOR

WARNER BROS. MAKE IT LIVE AGAIN TO THRILL YOU AS FEW MOTION PICTURES EVER HAVE!

One of the biggest casts ever amassed for one production – starring

ERROL FLYNN · OLIVIA deHAVILLAND

BASIL RATHBONE · CLAUDE RAINS

ALAN HALE · EUGENE PALLETTE

DIRECTED BY MICHAEL CURTIZ and WILLIAM KEIGHLEY

Original Screen Play by Norman Reilly Raine and Seton I. Miller · Based Upon Ancient Robin Hood Legends · Music by Erich Wolfgang Korngold

REISSUED — — GREAT PICTURES ARE FOREVER NEW!

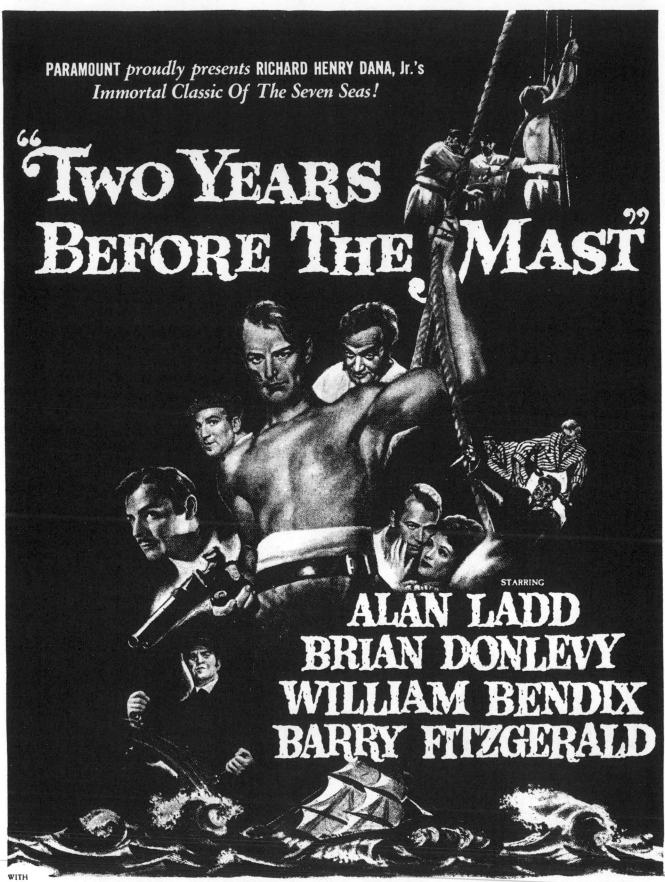

PARAMOUNT *proudly presents* RICHARD HENRY DANA, Jr.'s
Immortal Classic Of The Seven Seas!

"TWO YEARS BEFORE THE MAST"

STARRING

ALAN LADD
BRIAN DONLEVY
WILLIAM BENDIX
BARRY FITZGERALD

WITH
Howard da SILVA · Esther FERNANDEZ · Albert DEKKER · Luis VAN ROOTEN · Darryl HICKMAN
Produced by SETON I. MILLER · Directed by JOHN FARROW · Screen Play by Seton I. Miller and George Bruce

No one comes close to JAMES BOND 007

ALBERT R. BROCCOLI presents
ROGER MOORE
as IAN FLEMING'S
JAMES BOND 007
in FOR YOUR EYES ONLY

Starring CAROLE BOUQUET • TOPOL • LYNN-HOLLY JOHNSON • JULIAN GLOVER
Produced by ALBERT R. BROCCOLI • Directed by JOHN GLEN
Screenplay by RICHARD MAIBAUM and MICHAEL G. WILSON • Executive Producer MICHAEL G. WILSON
Music by BILL CONTI • Production Designer PETER LAMONT
Associate·Producer TOM PEVSNER   PANAVISION® TECHNICOLOR®

ORIGINAL MOTION PICTURE SOUNDTRACK
ON LIBERTY RECORDS AND TAPES

PG PARENTAL GUIDANCE SUGGESTED
SOME MATERIAL MAY NOT BE SUITABLE FOR CHILDREN

DOLBY STEREO™
IN SELECTED THEATRES

COPYRIGHT © MCMLXXXI DANJAQ S.A.
ALL RIGHTS RESERVED

United Artists
A Transamerica Company

Title Song Performed by SHEENA EASTON

Biography

Whether they were about inventors, songwriters, statesmen, sports figures, or just plain celebrities, Hollywood invariably found them worthy of individual biographical treatment on the screen. Actually, there was very little concern about the quality of the character involved, nor was too much attention given to whether that person actually lived the kind of life that would translate into good cinema. Hollywood screen biographies traditionally bear little or no relation to real life, especially to the life of the person involved. If there had been insufficient conflict, then some contention was simply invented; if there had been no real love interest, no beautiful women, no handsome men, no matter—they were merely created from whole cloth and inserted at the proper moment.

As film, these biographies were usually sold to the movie-going public on the strength of the person or persons portrayed, although some were only vehicles for a particular star. Nearly always, there was at least the reliance on a major "name" star to add to the box office appeal.

Madame Curie (1943) purported to be based on the life of the famous scientist, starred Greer Garson and Walter Pidgeon. The two had been co-starred in the wildly popular *Mrs. Miniver,* so this second pairing was M-G-M's attempt to parlay their popularity into more box office gold. Certainly, the ad gave the uninformed reader no indication of the film's content, featuring as it did the likenesses of the two stars, their names in very large type, and a reminder that if you liked them in *Mrs. Miniver,* you're going to love them in this one.

Although the ad for *The Great Caruso* (1950) gave Mario Lanza and his co-star Ann Blyth equal billing as far as line credits were concerned, the movie was definitely Lanza's. It was a simple case of the studio finding a film subject suitable to the specific talents of a handsome tenor who had a great screen personality. What could be a more natural subject than the most famous operatic tenor of all time? That the movie had very little to do with the real story of Caruso's life made little difference; only the bare bones of a plot was required—the rest would be singing. The result was a straightforward star vehicle. Accordingly, the ad featured Lanza's likeness in many guises—smiling, singing, romancing. Visually it was somewhat busy, but it was an effective approach in reaching Lanza's fans.

The life of another singer was brought to the screen in *The Helen Morgan Story* (1957). Once again Ann Blyth was starred in the title role. This film, however, was not a star vehicle; the moviemakers were selling a story, and the ads promised that they had plenty to tell. Working on the questionable assumption that a large part of the audience had never heard of Helen Morgan, the creators of this ad went to great lengths to indicate that this story dealt with the seamy side of life. The film was not very successful. It is most notable today for the presence of the young Paul Newman, and for the songs which were dubbed by the underrated singer, Gogi Grant.

Lon Chaney, the famous silent screen actor, was the *Man of a Thousand Faces* (1957). He was a difficult subject to capture because the general audience knew little or nothing of his life. They knew him—if at all—as an actor famous for his disguises, for his grisly yet somehow touching portrayals of such figures of horror as Quasimodo in *The Hunchback of Notre Dame,* and the title character in *The Phantom of the Opera.* The ad for this biographical film was quite direct and true to the film, yet it was oddly static and unappealing. It was difficult to know how best to sell this movie, which seemed to exist primarily to provide James Cagney with an opportunity to give a bravura performance. Despite the presence of Dorothy Malone, the movie and the ad were distinctly lacking in sex appeal. The movie-going audience did not respond.

Audiences did respond, however, to *The Glenn Miller Story,* a typically saccharine, yet very lively and appealing movie chronicling the life of the famous bandleader. Made in 1953, it starred two very popular performers—James Stewart and June Allyson. It featured lots of Miller's music; it was nostalgic, romantic, and uplifting. As a result, the movie scored a major success and sparked a revival of Glenn Miller's music. The ad was simple and direct, selling the title figure, its two main stars and a lot of tickets.

Gary Cooper was another extremely popular star, and his performance in *The Pride of the Yankees* (1942) was one of the most successful and enduring in his long career. Lou Gehrig, the subject of the film, was a popular and successful baseball figure who fought a long, losing battle with a devastating crippling disease. Lou's struggle captured the attention of an audience well beyond the normal realm of sports fans. The movie was well crafted, and its success was virtually assured by the combination of subject and star. As with *The Glenn Miller Story,* all the ad agency had to do was announce to a waiting public that Gary Cooper would portray Lou Gehrig, and the lines began to form.

The ad for *Somebody Up There Likes Me* (1956), while graphically very striking, is something of a puzzlement. The two principal performers—Paul Newman and Pier Angeli—though popular at the time, were not yet stars of any great significance. The subject of the film was Rocky Graziano, a popular boxer who overcame many hurdles to become a champion fighter. However, nowhere is there a mention of boxing in the ad, and, in fact, one has to read through nearly all the credits to even find Graziano's name! What the ad seems to have been selling was an inspirational title and some sense that this film is "important." The film was quite gritty, even bleak,

but there was an emotional payoff. Ultimately, the film succeeded, and did much to advance the popularity of Paul Newman.

The Nun's Story (1959) was also a very successful film, based on the best-selling book by Kathryn Hulme. Audrey Hepburn was at the height of her popularity, and was a perfect choice to portray a young woman who could not live within the severely restricted world of the Catholic convent. The ad, designed rather loosely in the shape of a cross, relied heavily on Miss Hepburn's appeal. It also did much to suggest a sense of adventure and conflict, perhaps in an effort to allay the misgivings of some moviegoers who might find the title and the subject matter slanted too heavily toward the inspirational.

The ad for *Young Mr. Lincoln* (1939) suffered from a split personality. Visually it was reverential in approach with only one minor exception: all the characters are depicted with decidedly stern countenances. Yet the copy is in direct conflict, telling of Lincoln's ". . . thrilling, exciting, romantic youth . . ." promising a picture astir with ". . . drama, romance, action, emotion!" It's almost as though the people who did the art and those who wrote the copy had seen two different movies! Basically, they were selling a character, young Mr. Lincoln, and a star, Henry Fonda. Directed by John Ford, the film has found a lasting audience.

Stanley and Livingstone (1939) was based, ever so vaguely, on actual events in the lives of real people. In many ways it was *the* typical Hollywood bio-film, taking great liberties with fact in order to make the story fit the big screen. The ad promised action, adventure, some romance, and a strong performance by its star, Spencer Tracy. In its own muddled way, the movie delivered what it promised. Moreover, it succeeded at the time, and endures today as a staple of late night television.

Biographical films have changed only slightly over the years. Perhaps there is more of an effort today to achieve reality in terms of atmosphere, but the facts themselves remain subject to alteration in an effort to heighten the drama. And, as always, these films are sold either on the strength of the subject or the appeal of the star playing the pivotal role. Occasionally, as with *Coal Miner's Daughter,* the two strengths come together to create a film of major importance.

Helen Morgan—her songs—her sins.

"Look, I watched you tonight. You couldn't take your eyes off me. That's why I'm here."

HOW COULD THIS HAPPEN TO A GIRL LIKE HELEN MORGAN?

Helen Morgan sat on a piano – and no star ever climbed higher.
Helen Morgan fell in love – and no woman ever fell lower . . . !
Her real story – from real life – the story no one has told before!
There was only one Helen Morgan – there's only one

the Helen Morgan Story

PRESENTED BY WARNER BROS. STARRING **ANN BLYTH · PAUL NEWMAN** · RICHARD CARLSON
ALSO STARRING GENE EVANS · ALAN KING · CARA WILLIAMS · Written by OSCAR SAUL, DEAN RIESNER, STEPHEN LONGSTREET, NELSON GIDDING
Musical Numbers Staged by LeROY PRINZ · Produced by MARTIN RACKIN · Directed by MICHAEL CURTIZ

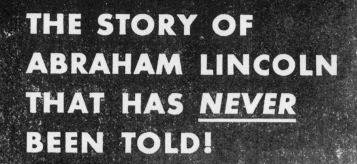

THE STORY OF ABRAHAM LINCOLN THAT HAS <u>NEVER</u> BEEN TOLD!

Two boys charged with murder . . . and between them and the gallows . . . the youthful backwoods attorney for the defense . . . ABE LINCOLN!

His thrilling, exciting, romantic youth . . . wrestling, fighting, telling funny stories, falling in love! A picture stirring with its drama, romance, action, emotion!

Twentieth Century-Fox presents

DARRYL F. ZANUCK'S production of

YOUNG Mr. LINCOLN

with

HENRY FONDA · ALICE BRADY · MARJORIE WEAVER · ARLEEN WHELAN

EDDIE COLLINS · PAULINE MOORE
RICHARD CROMWELL · DONALD MEEK
JUDITH DICKENS · EDDIE QUILLAN

A Cosmopolitan Production
Directed by John Ford

Associate Producer Kenneth Macgowan
Original Screen Play by Lamar Trotti

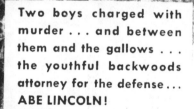

Mr. and Mrs. Miniver ....together again!

GREER GARSON
WALTER PIDGEON

give their best performance in their best picture

MADAME CURIE

Directed by MERVYN LeROY Produced by SIDNEY FRANKLIN

Presented by M.G.M.

With a brilliant supporting cast, Henry Travers, Robert Walker, Dame May Whitty, Elsa Basserman, Van Johnson, Albert Basserman, C. Aubrey Smith, Victor Francen, Reginald Owen, Margaret O'Brien · Screen Play by Paul Osborn and Paul H. Rameau. Based on the book, "Madame Curie" by Eve Curie. A METRO-GOLDWYN-MAYER PICTURE

"Africa holds a hundred nameless dangers! Fever... heat... cannibals... jungle...!"

"Darling, I beg you... make Stanley turn back... before it's too late!"

"Death shall not seal the secrets Livingstone knows! We go on until we find him!"

"*Dr. Livingstone, I presume?*" The famous words of Stanley... an unforgettable thrill!

Twentieth Century-Fox
presents
Darryl F. Zanuck's Production
of

STANLEY *and* LIVINGSTONE

with the finest acting cast
ever assembled!

Another masterful performance by SPENCER TRACY ... twice winner of the Academy Award!

starring

SPENCER   NANCY   RICHARD
TRACY · KELLY · GREENE

Walter Brennan · Charles Coburn · Sir Cedric
Hardwicke · Henry Hull · Henry Travers

Directed by Henry King

Associate Producer Kenneth Macgowan · Screen Play by
Philip Dunne and Julien Josephson · Historical Research
and Story Outline by Hal Long and Sam Hellman

THE GREATEST ADVENTURE KNOWN TO MAN!

On this fateful autumn day,
the nun called Sister Luke
under special and extraordinary
circumstances was forever
released from all her vows.

She left her convent because
in her own words she was
no longer a true nun. And
her story swiftly
became the most
gripping and
dramatic personal
story of this
decade.

WARNER BROS. *presents*

AUDREY HEPBURN

as Sister Luke, who was not like the others

IN FRED ZINNEMANN'S
PRODUCTION OF

THE NUN'S STORY

TECHNICOLOR®

CO-STARRING

PETER FINCH

*as the cynical Congo
Surgeon. Dr. Fortunati*

All the
human
depth and
electrifying
drama of the
tremendous
best-seller!

FILMED IN BELGIUM, ITALY, AFRICA
— AND MOSTLY IN THE CONSCIENCE OF
A YOUNG AND BEAUTIFUL GIRL!

ALSO-STARRING
DAME EDITH EVANS DAME PEGGY ASHCROFT DEAN JAGGER with MILDRED DUNNOCK SCREENPLAY BY ROBERT ANDERSON
FROM THE BOOK BY KATHRYN C HULME PRODUCED BY HENRY BLANKE DIRECTED BY FRED ZINNEMANN MUSIC COMPOSED AND CONDUCTED BY FRANZ WAXMAN

MORE LOVE SONGS FROM THE STAR WHO THRILLED AMERICA WITH "BE MY LOVE"!

Golden-voiced Mario Lanza enraptures millions of movie-lovers in the role he was destined to play . . . the love story of the fabulous Caruso, gallery god of his era . . . who sang his way from cafes to fame . . . and into the hearts of the world's most glamorous women!

"A NEW IDOL! THE HOTTEST SINGER TO HIT THE SOUND TRACK IN A DECADE!"
—*says Time Magazine*

M-G-M
"The Best in Musicals"
presents

"The Great" CARUSO

COLOR BY
TECHNICOLOR

STARRING

MARIO LANZA ★ ANN BLYTH
DOROTHY KIRSTEN ★ JARMILA NOVOTNA
BLANCHE THEBOM

THE IDOL OF MILLIONS! In two short years, Lanza has swept to the pinnacle of Hollywood stardom! Now he has won the coveted role of Caruso!

COAST-TO-COAST TRIUMPH! Lanza's voice and charm have won him acclaim and adulation such as only Caruso has ever known before!

WITH
TERESA CELLI · RICHARD HAGEMAN · CARL BENTON REID
Written by Sonya Levien and William Ludwig ★ *Suggested by Dorothy Caruso's Biography of her Husband*
Directed by RICHARD THORPE ★ Produced by JOE PASTERNAK ★ Associate Producer JESSE L. LASKY
A Metro-Goldwyn-Mayer Picture

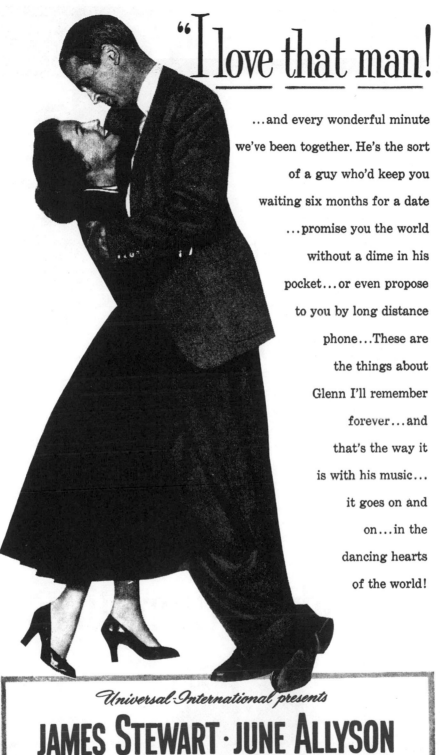

"I love that man!

...and every wonderful minute we've been together. He's the sort of a guy who'd keep you waiting six months for a date ...promise you the world without a dime in his pocket...or even propose to you by long distance phone...These are the things about Glenn I'll remember forever...and that's the way it is with his music... it goes on and on...in the dancing hearts of the world!

Universal-International presents

JAMES STEWART · JUNE ALLYSON
The GLENN MILLER STORY

COLOR BY *Technicolor*

HEAR THESE MEMORABLE GLENN MILLER HITS:

"MOONLIGHT SERENADE"
"LITTLE BROWN JUG"
"IN THE MOOD"
"PENNSYLVANIA 6-5000"
"STRING OF PEARLS"
"TUXEDO JUNCTION"
"CHATTANOOGA CHOO CHOO"
and many, many more!

with

CHARLES DRAKE · GEORGE TOBIAS · HENRY MORGAN
and these Musical "Greats" as Guest Stars!
FRANCES LANGFORD · LOUIS ARMSTRONG · GENE KRUPA
BEN POLLACK · THE MODERNAIRES

Directed by ANTHONY MANN · Written by VALENTINE DAVIES and OSCAR BRODNEY · Produced by AARON ROSENBERG

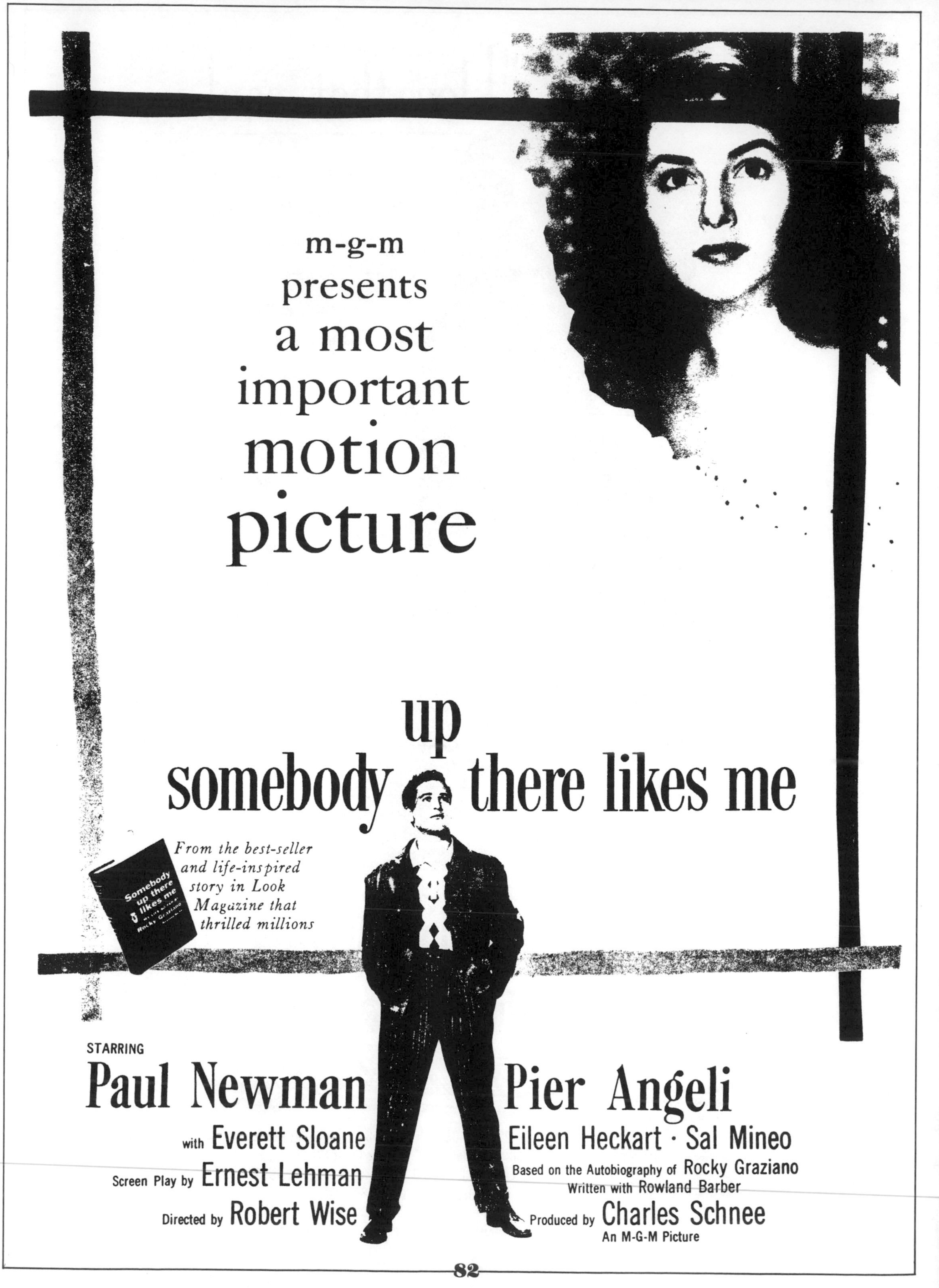

m-g-m
presents
a most
important
motion
picture
somebody up there likes me
From the best-seller
and life-inspired
story in Look
Magazine that
thrilled millions
Somebody up there likes me
STARRING
Paul Newman
Pier Angeli
with Everett Sloane
Eileen Heckart · Sal Mineo
Screen Play by Ernest Lehman
Based on the Autobiography of Rocky Graziano
Written with Rowland Barber
Directed by Robert Wise
Produced by Charles Schnee
An M-G-M Picture

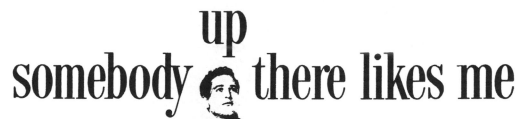

This is the man — Lon Chaney...

and these ... are his thousand faces!

This is the woman he loved...

...and this is the woman he hated!

Universal-International presents

JAMES CAGNEY
as the fabulous **LON CHANEY**
DOROTHY MALONE

JANE GREER

...and this is the story that lay hidden from the world behind the magic of his make-up!

CinemaScope

"MAN OF A THOUSAND FACES"

with
MARJORIE RAMBEAU • JIM BACKUS • ROGER SMITH
Screenplay by R. WRIGHT CAMPBELL, IVAN GOFF and BEN ROBERTS
Story by RALPH WHEELWRIGHT
Directed by JOSEPH PEVNEY • Produced by ROBERT ARTHUR

UNIVERSAL'S SPECIAL RELEASE FOR HOLLYWOOD'S GOLDEN JUBILEE

Private life
OF THE MAN MILLIONS CHEERED!

Here's the intimate story of a man millions idolized. He fought his way to the top—and then he met Her! Together they reveled in life and love. But there was one secret they tried to keep from each other—and out of their struggle comes one of the screen's most dramatic and touching romances. Presented by Samuel Goldwyn, who gave you some of the finest films you've ever seen.

SAMUEL GOLDWYN presents

GARY COOPER
in
THE PRIDE OF THE YANKEES
(THE LIFE OF LOU GEHRIG)

with

TERESA WRIGHT • **BABE RUTH** • **WALTER BRENNAN**

VELOZ and YOLANDA • RAY NOBLE and his Orchestra • Directed by SAM WOOD
Screen Play by Jo Swerling and Herman J. Mankiewicz
Original Story by Paul Gallico • Released through
RKO Radio Pictures Inc.

It's the Great American Story!

WATCH FOR IT AT
YOUR LOCAL THEATRE

War

Appropriately, war films reached the height of their popularity during the 1940s. The films of this genre made during World War II were heroic—patriotic portraits of brave men and women fighting to rid the world of madmen. The villains were obvious; there was nothing ambiguous about who was good and who was evil. The films made following the war were a little more introspective. They dealt more with the emotions of the soldier and of the women left behind. Few of these movies were actively anti-war, but they did not glorify the soldier or the war effort as the earlier films had.

During the Korean conflict there was a resurgence of war films, but only a few were purely unquestioning, patriotic efforts. The war in Vietnam produced almost no pro-war movies—it was an unpopular war, one that many Americans were totally against; people simply did not want to see movies about this war, they just wanted it to go away.

Made just prior to the start of World War II, *Flight Command* (1941) was concerned with American naval air power. The movie is significant primarily because it was in that same year that the U.S. Naval fleet—including its air force—was dealt such a devastating blow at Pearl Harbor. It was not a particularly successful film, despite the fact that it starred the very popular Robert Taylor, whose name was featured above the title. The ad and the picture relied on Taylor's popularity, promising little else, although the copy mentioned "romance" and "beauties." Had it come out a few months later, the movie might have been more successful, but in early 1941 there was still sufficient anti-war sentiment in America

to keep the public from warming to the subject.

Destroyer also was not very successful. It was just one of many war films released in 1943, and was of no special distinction. The ad, however, is quite typical of the genre, and is strikingly different from *Flight Command* in its approach. The United States was now at war. The ad, therefore, promised lots of action—at sea, in this case some romance, and a happy ending. In a film such as this, although the war was far from being won, there was never any question of the ultimate outcome. Edward G. Robinson was one of Hollywood's few leading men not called into war service, so he portrayed a rather unlikely ship's captain. Glenn Ford and Marguerite Chapman provided the love interest. The ad copy would have had one believe that the principal conflict here was not the war but the bizarre triangle involving a man's love for his wife and for his ship.

Also released in 1943, *Crash Dive* was heralded as Tyrone Power's "farewell role for the duration." Power's name was above the title, and the visuals portrayed him in a number of ways: he was shown in battle action, in an embrace with Ann Baxter, and as being just plain beautiful in his uniform. Also, according to this ad, the movie was not just filmed in technicolor, but "in stirring Technicolor." It was not an especially distinguished movie, but it did enjoy moderate success, primarily because of its star.

Paul Muni's star was on the wane in 1945, when *Counter-Attack* was released. The ad was rather nonspecific—promising "tenseness!" "bigness!" and "suspense!" It was difficult to determine just what the whole thing was all about. Muni and promises of excitement were not enough—the film was a failure at the box office.

By 1950 there had been enough time for a considerable amount of post-war disillusionment to set in. Books such as *The Naked and the Dead* and *The Young Lions* graphically depicted the horrors of war, the destruction of mankind and of individual men and women. Movies like *The Men* and *The Best Years of Our Lives* demanded that Americans understand just what the conflict had done to society and to those who had only half survived. Despite these heavy doses of negative reality, films such as *Twelve O'Clock High* continued to be produced. While it was not a glorification of war, it was a straightforward depiction of the events leading up to the dropping of the atomic bomb on Japan. Gregory Peck was very popular at the box office, and was therefore the main feature of the ad. The movie was well made and proved to be successful.

Battle Cry (1955) was a totally different kind of war film. As the copy for the movie ad stated, it was a picture "about young people in love when the battle is far away," and certainly the graphics for the ad carried through with the notion of love—or, more precisely, sex. No scenes of battle were depicted; instead there were pictures of the stars in various beef- and cheese-cake poses. In this case, clearly it was sex, not war, that Hollywood was selling. The novel by Leon Uris had been controversial and successful; so was the film.

The Bold and the Brave (1956) was an attempt to show in realistic terms the effects of war on the young men who fought and suffered. The ad suggested romance and battle scenes, and featured the four principal characters. Despite some good performances (Mickey Rooney was nominated for an Academy Award for his work in the film), the movie was not a success with the public. The Korean conflict had only recently ended; perhaps the American public was a bit war weary.

In 1955, two wildly popular stars managed to make a success of *The Bridges at Toko-Ri.*

William Holden had won the Academy Award only two years earlier for his role in *Stalag 16,* and Grace Kelly had won an Oscar in 1954 for *The Country Wife.* The ad for *Toko-Ri* promised a love story, featuring the two stars in a warm—although certainly not passionate—embrace. Based on the novella by James Michener, the film dealt with the Korean conflict, still fresh in the minds of the public. But in this movie, it was the human interest, not the war, that was paramount.

The war in Vietnam was not a time for heroes; it was not a conflict that lent itself to the celebration of individual valor. *Apocalypse Now* was Francis Ford Coppola's surrealistic vision of the madness of a war that no one knew how to win, yet no one had the power to stop. Appropriately, the ads did not picture scenes of battle, nor were there pictures of couples clinging together for support in the face of terror and distress. It was an ugly film, yet frighteningly powerful and was entirely the director's vision.

Robert De Niro was the star and main selling point of *The Deer Hunter.* The film turned out to be a huge success both critically and financially, independent of its cast, winning the Academy Award as best picture of 1978. It presented a very real, horrific vision of war and its effect on a group of men from middle America. *The Deer Hunter* was a startlingly realistic film, using a symbolic title and ad approach. It was a contradiction that worked remarkably well.

As noted earlier, there seems to be little market for war films today. Even the better war films made during the 1940s and 1950s seem to have lost their appeal, for they are shown with less frequency on television and are seldom featured in movie house retrospectives. Perhaps another war, one more popular than the Vietnam conflict, will see a rise in military patriotism, but hopefully the war film is a genre that is gone forever, a genre that will exist as a kind of macabre nostalgia.

FRANCIS FORD COPPOLA
PRESENTS

MARLON BRANDO   ROBERT DUVALL   MARTIN SHEEN in APOCALYPSE NOW
FREDERIC FORREST   ALBERT HALL   SAM BOTTOMS   LARRY FISHBURNE and DENNIS HOPPER
Produced and Directed by FRANCIS COPPOLA
Written by JOHN MILIUS and FRANCIS COPPOLA
Co-Produced by FRED ROOS, GRAY FREDERICKSON and TOM STERNBERG
Director of Photography VITTORIO STORARO   Production Designer DEAN TAVOULARIS   Editor RICHARD MARKS
Sound Design by WALTER MURCH   Music by CARMINE COPPOLA and FRANCIS COPPOLA

A STORY
OF TWELVE
MEN AS
THEIR
WOMEN
NEVER
KNEW
THEM...

...of one man who
stood forward—alone!
GREGORY PECK in
his most exciting role—as
"Savage," who crosses
wings with Destiny!

Darryl F. Zanuck
presents

THE WORLD
STANDS STILL
AT...

TWELVE O'CLOCK HIGH

starring

GREGORY PECK

20th
CENTURY-FOX

with
HUGH MARLOWE · GARY MERRILL · MILLARD MITCHELL · DEAN JAGGER · ROBERT ARTHUR · PAUL STEWART · JOHN KELLOGG · BOB PATTEN

Produced by DARRYL F. ZANUCK   Directed by HENRY KING

Screen Play by Sy Bartlett and Beirne Lay, Jr. · Based on the Novel by Sy Bartlett and Beirne Lay, Jr.

Tomorrow, the deadliest mission ...tonight, the greatest love!

Two of today's most exciting stars teamed in a love story you'll remember forever!

William Holden as Lt. Brubaker, who'd done more than his share!

Fredric March as the Admiral, big brass ... with a heart of gold!

JAMES A. MICHENER'S

THE BRIDGES AT TOKO-RI

A Perlberg-Seaton production
in color by
TECHNICOLOR

The mighty love and adventure drama from the novel that millions thrilled to in LIFE magazine by James A. Michener, Pulitzer Prize winning author of "South Pacific"!

Grace Kelly as Nancy, who followed her man to the ends of the earth!

Mickey Rooney as Mike, the 'copter pilot, all fun — and fearlessness!

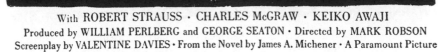

With ROBERT STRAUSS • CHARLES McGRAW • KEIKO AWAJI
Produced by WILLIAM PERLBERG and GEORGE SEATON • Directed by MARK ROBSON
Screenplay by VALENTINE DAVIES • From the Novel by James A. Michener • A Paramount Picture

• • •

WORLD PREMIERE AT NEW YORK'S RADIO CITY MUSIC HALL
AND SOON IN LEADING THEATRES THROUGHOUT THE COUNTRY!

The
guys of
'Battle Cry'

Hodge and the night he learned the sordid truth about **Rae**

The
girls of
'Battle Cry'

Andy and his reckless love that brought the trouble to **Patricia**

The
scorchingly
personal
story of

"Ski" and his revenge for the heartbreak caused by **Susan**

"Battle Cry"

Danny whose devotion to Kathy almost melted in the arms of **Elaine**

THE BEST-SELLER
THE NATION
COULDN'T
PUT DOWN—
ABOUT
YOUNG
PEOPLE
IN LOVE
WHEN
THE BATTLE
IS FAR AWAY...

'Spanish Joe' and his name for anybody's girl... **Babe**

PRESENTED BY WARNER BROS. IN **CINEMASCOPE** WarnerColor · Stereophonic Sound

STARRING
VAN ☆ ALDO ☆ MONA ☆ NANCY ☆ JAMES ☆ RAYMOND ☆ TAB ☆ DOROTHY ☆ ANNE
HEFLIN ☆ RAY ☆ FREEMAN ☆ OLSON ☆ WHITMORE ☆ MASSEY ☆ HUNTER ☆ MALONE ☆ FRANCIS

SCREEN PLAY BY
LEON M. URIS
DIRECTED BY
RAOUL WALSH

ORIGINAL MUSIC BY MAX STEINER

HER ONLY RIVAL IS HIS SHIP!

"You feel toward a ship as you do toward a woman when you marry her... You take her for better or you take her for worse ... and you don't leave her when the going gets tough!"

For man-to-man thrills and *just plain GUTS* IT STANDS ALONE!

DESTROYER

STARRING
EDWARD G. ROBINSON

Glenn Ford · Marguerite Chapman · Edgar Buchanan

with

Screen Play by Frank Wead, Lewis Meltzer and Borden Chase · Produced by LOUIS F. EDELMAN
Directed by WILLIAM A. SEITER · A COLUMBIA PICTURE

With the Gratefully Acknowledged Cooperation of the

★ UNITED STATES NAVY ★

METRO-GOLDWYN-MAYER

presents

ROBERT TAYLOR
in
FLIGHT COMMAND

THE FASTEST THING ON FILM!

THE PICTURE OF THE MONTH!

Ever since M·G·M gave to the public its memorable production "Hell Divers", this famed studio has sought a drama equally thrilling and romantic, with a spectacular background of America's fighting ships of the air. Here it is, surpassing highest hopes for a successor! It is the story of the "Hell Cats" of the Navy's Armada of the skies...excitingly filmed at Pensacola, San Diego and Pearl Harbor... a romance of air-devils and the beauties who love them...a picture that will electrify America with its breath-taking unfolding!

WITH RUTH HUSSEY ★ WALTER PIDGEON

PAUL KELLY • SHEPPARD STRUDWICK • NAT PENDLETON

A FRANK BORZAGE PRODUCTION

Screen Play by Wells Root and Commander Harvey Haislip
Directed by Frank Borzage • Produced by J. Walter Ruben

WALTER PIDGEON
as the Commander
and...
RUTH HUSSEY
as the girl who made
the "Hell Cats" purr!

★ ★

You will **never** live a more sinister drama...nor a more exciting one!

COLUMBIA PICTURES
presents

PAUL MUNI

in

COUNTER-ATTACK

(Adapted from the BROADWAY STAGE SUCCESS)

Thrilling with tenseness!
Towering with bigness!
Startling with suspense!

with

MARGUERITE   LARRY
CHAPMAN · PARKS

Screen Play by John Howard Lawson
Directed by ZOLTAN KORDA

His farewell role for the duration!

TYRONE POWER

Leading a reckless crew on the war's most daring mission! Battling death in a depth-bombed submarine! Blasting Nazis on a bold Commando raid! Finding love in precious, stolen moments!

CRASHING HIS WAY TO UNFORGETTABLE GLORY in

CRASH DIVE

IN STIRRING TECHNICOLOR

with
ANNE   DANA
BAXTER · ANDREWS

James GLEASON · Dame May WHITTY

20th CENTURY-FOX PICTURE

Directed by ARCHIE MAYO
Produced by MILTON SPERLING
Screen Play by Jo Swerling · Original Story by W. R. Burnett

ROBERT DE NIRO

A MICHAEL CIMINO FILM

UNIVERSAL PICTURES
and
EMI FILMS
present
"THE DEER HUNTER"
Co-starring

JOHN CAZALE · JOHN SAVAGE · MERYL STREEP · CHRISTOPHER WALKEN

Music by STANLEY MYERS   Editor PETER ZINNER

Director of Photography VILMOS ZSIGMOND, A.S.C.

Production Consultant JOANN CARELLI   Produced by BARRY SPIKINGS,
MICHAEL DEELEY, MICHAEL CIMINO and JOHN PEVERALL
Story by MICHAEL CIMINO & DERIC WASHBURN and LOUIS GARFINKLE
& QUINN K. REDEKER   Screenplay by DERIC WASHBURN

Directed by MICHAEL CIMINO   A UNIVERSAL RELEASE EMI TECHNICOLOR® PANAVISION®

Now a JOVE Book   □□ DOLBY ®STEREO   ©1978 UNIVERSAL CITY STUDIOS INC ALL RIGHTS RESERVED   R RESTRICTED

The story of events that made a bold woman out of a lovely young girl... and brave fighting men out of boys who played at living!

IRVING H. LEVIN presents

The BOLD and the BRAVE

breath-taking as a one-man tank battle...

impassioned as its war-weary lovers... an unforgettable experience!

starring

| WENDELL **COREY** | MICKEY **ROONEY** | DON **TAYLOR** | NICOLE **MAUREY** |

with **JOHN SMITH · RACE GENTRY**   *SUPERSCOPE*   A HAL E. CHESTER Production
Directed by LEWIS R. FOSTER
Story and Screenplay by ROBERT LEWIN

Western

In recent years, the Western film has fallen into disfavor. There are still many classic Westerns which are shown in repertoire houses, and many other not-so-classic ones appear with frequency on television. But there have been few Westerns produced by Hollywood of late, and almost none have succeeded.

Perhaps part of the problem lies with the way movies are created today. In the halcyon days of the studios, Westerns were low-cost productions which were ground out on a regular basis. They seldom meant high returns, but they virtually never lost money, and they provided the studios with a showcase for developing new young talent, as well as enabling directors to develop their own personal style at low financial risk.

One such director was John Ford. His masculine, no-nonsense approach to film was perfectly suited to the Western, and he found his perfect star in John Wayne. The two were paired in many films, two of which are represented in this collection of ads. The ad for *She Wore a Yellow Ribbon* (1949) headlined "In the John Ford Tradition of Greatness," and it featured a large likeness of the uncharacteristically-mustachioed John Wayne. It promised action and style, and moviegoers knew they would not be disappointed.

The Searchers (1956) was not a traditional shoot-'em-up Western, but it was another wonderful variation on the genre. Again it paired John Ford and John Wayne, and once again it was a very successful film. The ad in this instance played up the theme of the movie, the search for a young girl stolen by Indians. It was visually arresting and most effective.

Howard Hawks was a remarkably versatile di-

rector. It's hard to believe that the same man was the creative force behind such diverse films as the screwball comedy *Bringing Up Baby* and the classic Western *Red River*. Hawks directed a number of films of both genres, as well as films which are best classified as straight drama. Just about all his films were successful. *Rio Bravo* was a widely popular film in 1959. Once again, John Wayne was starred, but featured with him—symptomatic of the changing times—were a popular singer, Dean Martin, and a teen idol, Ricky Nelson, also a singer of sorts and anachronistically described in the ad as "The Rockin' baby-faced Kid." The ad campaign relied heavily on the personality and box office appeal of the three stars, but the film stands today as a classic, primarily on the strength of vision of the creator behind it.

Another director who made a number of memorable Westerns was Raoul Walsh. He was best in outdoor, action films, to which he always lent a touch of genuine tenderness. *Along the Great Divide,* made in 1951, was a fine movie, but it found very little popular acceptance. Perhaps part of the problem lies in the approach taken in the ad for this film. Except for the reference to "law-man" in one of the ad lines, and the landscape showing mountains on the horizon, there is little evidence that this is a Western. Certainly the selling line, "Warner Bros. Bring You Romance That Avalanches from the Top of the Adventure World!," is nonspecific, and the ad generally emphasized the two principal stars, Kirk Douglas and Virginia Mayo, neither of them known particularly as Western stars.

Gunfight at the O.K. Corral was more ambitious than most Westerns. It dealt with the friendship between Wyatt Earp, lawman, and Doc Holliday, outlaw. Released in 1957, the film was extremely popular. Kirk Douglas was again starred along with Burt Lancaster. The ad for this film is particularly good, depicting the two main characters in action, as well as giving a montage of action sequences, combined with copy that told just enough of the plot to make it appealing.

Movie ads of the 1930s tended to be exceedingly busy, and the ad for *Jesse James* (1939) was no exception. As a movie, it was extremely popular, despite the fact that the story was unbelievably fictionalized. It boasted two major box office draws in Tyrone Power and Henry Fonda, both of whom were prominently featured in the ad. It was a big-budget Western and it paid off handsomely, enhancing the popularity of both stars. Neither was known as Western actors, although both had appeared in several such films. Fonda, in fact, appeared the following year in a sequel to this movie entitled *The Return of Frank James.*

The Tin Star, made in 1957, also featured Henry Fonda. It was one of the "new breed" of Westerns, movies in which posses and gunfights were less crucial to the plot than was the psychological make-up of the protagonist. Action was secondary to motivation. These films were indicative of the unsettled, questioning attitudes of the times. The ad for *The Tin Star* reflects this change in tone: it is reserved and undramatic; there are no scenes of gunfighting, no horses galloping across rugged horizons.

Westerns traditionally have been the domain of men—rugged, brawny, quick to fight, men portrayed by stars like John Wayne, Gary Cooper or Clint Eastwood. There were women in the old West, of course, but they were seldom celebrated in film. *Arizona* (1941) was something of an exception. It starred Jean Arthur, a popular actress known primarily for her portrayals of vivacious, often oddball, unpretentious heroines in a string of social comedies. In 1937 she had assayed the role of Calamity Jane in the film called *The Plainsman,* so she was actually no stranger to the genre. *Arizona* was very popular. The ad, a particularly attractive one, was straightforward and effective—Miss Arthur was featured against a montage of action scenes which served to reassure the viewer that despite the sex of the protagonist, this was a Western in the traditional sense.

The ad for *Westward the Women* (1952)—a totally forgettable movie—seemed to have been selling sex. Robert Taylor was the star, but the subject of the film was the trek of 200 women across the country to meet the strangers they had contracted to marry. The ad copy allowed as how "some [of the women] were hussies in silk . . . forgetting the past," below which was featured the glamorous French actress Denise Darcel in a seductive pose. Not seductive enough, however, because the movie bombed at the box office.

The Outlaw was a *cause celebre* at the time of its production in 1940. Howard Hughes created the film as a vehicle for his new discovery, Jane Russell, a sultry, buxom brunette. But because of a phenomenal controversy which arose due to the showing of Miss Russell's cleavage, and one scene in which she bunked down with the title character in an effort to keep him warm, it was kept off the screen—except for a brief release in 1943—until 1950. The film, totally innocuous by today's standards, is notable primarily because of the ad campaign. Hughes was selling his star, with titillating promises of raunchy sex. If the film had been released in 1940, the campaign might have worked, but by 1950 no one cared.

And no one seems to care today, either. The nation has gone through a period of self-imposed guilt regarding the treatment of the native American Indians, so the naive films that showed the redmen as villians have no market. And while graphic violence is a favorite of contemporary movies, it seems to work better at the box office when presented in the context of a horror film or of a wild and destructive car chase. *Days of Heaven* is a case in point: a movie of total violence, it was a Western and died a much-publicized and celebrated death.

In The John Ford Tradition of Greatness

John Ford and Merian C. Cooper
present
JOHN WAYNE
JOANNE DRU
JOHN AGAR
BEN JOHNSON
HARRY CAREY, Jr.
in

JOHN WAYNE in his most heroic role as Captain Brittles of the U.S. Cavalry.

She Wore a Yellow Ribbon

with VICTOR McLAGLEN
MILDRED NATWICK · GEORGE O'BRIEN
ARTHUR SHIELDS
Directed by **JOHN FORD**
Story by JAMES WARNER BELLAH
Screen Play by FRANK NUGENT and LAURENCE STALLINGS
COLOR BY TECHNICOLOR
Produced by ARGOSY PICTURES CORPORATION   Distributed by RKO RADIO PICTURES

JOANNE DRU as Olivia | JOHN AGAR as Lt. Cohill | BEN JOHNSON as Tyree | HARRY CAREY, Jr. as Lt. Pennell | VICTOR McLAGLEN as Sgt. Quincannon | GEORGE O'BRIEN as Maj. Allshard

BURT LANCASTER · KIRK DOUGLAS

LAWMAN AND BADMAN...
THE STRANGEST FRIENDSHIP
THIS SIDE OF HEAVEN AND HELL!

...They fought shoulder to shoulder
in the wildest wide-open
stand-up gunfight in the history
of the West!

VISTAVISION

IN
HAL
WALLIS'
PRODUCTION OF

GUNFIGHT AT THE O.K. CORRAL

RHONDA FLEMING · JO VAN FLEET · JOHN IRELAND

co-starring

Directed by JOHN STURGES · Screenplay by LEON URIS · Music composed and conducted by DIMITRI TIOMKIN · A Paramount Picture

TECHNICOLOR®

The big guy with the battered hat...

The ragged woman-wrecked cast-off called Dude...

The rockin' baby-faced kid...

JOHN and DEAN and RICKY
WAYNE MARTIN NELSON

A *HOWARD HAWKS* PRODUCTION

They grew into giants at... **RIO BRAVO**

TECHNICOLOR®
from WARNER BROS.

...and the girl they all call "Feathers"

CO-STARRING
ANGIE DICKINSON · WALTER BRENNAN · WARD BOND · JOHN RUSSELL

WITH PEDRO GONZALEZ-GONZALEZ · ESTELITA RODRIGUEZ · Screenplay by JULES FURTHMAN and LEIGH BRACKETT
MUSIC COMPOSED AND CONDUCTED BY DIMITRI TIOMKIN · AN ARMADA PRODUCTION · Directed and Produced by HOWARD HAWKS

Hear Dean and Ricky Sing... "Rio Bravo" - "My Rifle, My Pony and Me" - "Cindy"!

"HE WAS AN OUTLAW...A KILLER...HIS LIFE WAS THE EPIC STORY OF A LAWLESS ERA!"

He was hunted, but he was human! And there was one—gentle yet dauntless—who flung her life away—into his arms!

The spectacular drama of the nation's most famous outlaw and the turbulent events that gave him to the world!

" Jesse, you're a hero now! But this will get into your blood! You'll turn into a killer and a wolf!"

"I know, but I hate the railroads, and when I hate, I have to do something about it!"

DARRYL F. ZANUCK'S
production of

JESSE JAMES

Photographed in **TECHNICOLOR**

starring

TYRONE POWER
HENRY FONDA
NANCY KELLY
RANDOLPH SCOTT
and HENRY HULL
SLIM SUMMERVILLE
J. EDWARD BROMBERG
BRIAN DONLEVY
JOHN CARRADINE
DONALD MEEK
JOHN RUSSELL
JANE DARWELL

Directed by Henry King
Associate Producer and Original
Screen Play by Nunnally Johnson
A 20th Century-Fox Picture

HE LED 200 WOMEN ON AN ADVENTURE THAT MOST MEN FEARED TO FACE!

WOMEN ... *finding a future!*

Each signed a contract to marry a man she selected from pictures of 200 homesteaders. And then faced a journey across the untamed Western wilderness ... to meet the stranger with whom she'd begin life anew!

THRILLINGLY AUTHENTIC!
Actually filmed on the California overland trail of '49!

WOMEN ... *forgetting the past!*

Some were hussies in silk ... who became heroines in calico. They defied Nature's fury, Indian attacks, a thousand perils and hardships ... and found the love they longed for at the end of the trail.

M-G-M presents

WESTWARD THE WOMEN

starring

ROBERT TAYLOR
DENISE DARCEL

HOPE EMERSON · JOHN McINTIRE

Screen Play by **CHARLES SCHNEE** Story by FRANK CAPRA

Directed by **WILLIAM A. WELLMAN** Produced by **DORE SCHARY**

An M-G-M Picture

TURBULENT ADVENTURE...SET AGAINST THE RICH, ROMANTIC TAPESTRY OF EARLY ARIZONA!

The story of lovely Phoebe Titus, titan of a woman, and her love for dashing Peter Muncie, Sergeant, U. S. A.! Mighty spectacle! Tempestuous stampedes! War! Lawless raids! Intrepid men and women! At last, in all its wild, brave magnificence, the motion picture drama of Arizona's birth!

Created by a great picture maker... at incalculable cost ... with a superb cast of thousands ... in especially re-created Old Tucson!

Wesley Ruggles'
ARIZONA
starring
JEAN ARTHUR
with
WILLIAM HOLDEN

WARREN WILLIAM · PORTER HALL
and a cast of thousands
Based on the Saturday Evening Post serial and novel by Clarence Budington Kelland
Screen play by Claude Binyon · Directed by WESLEY RUGGLES
A Columbia Picture

WATCH FOR THIS HIT PRODUCTION . . . AT YOUR LOCAL THEATRE

"Who's the prisoner now, law-man?"

Kirk
AS THE MAN
WHOSE HIDE
NO BULLET
COULD TOUCH...

Virginia
AS THE GIRL
WHO GOT UNDER
HIS SKIN!

WARNER BROS. BRING YOU NOW A ROMANCE THAT AVALANCHES FROM THE TOP OF THE ADVENTURE WORLD!

KIRK · VIRGINIA · JOHN · WALTER
DOUGLAS · MAYO · AGAR · BRENNAN
"ALONG THE GREAT DIVIDE"

DIRECTED BY
RAOUL WALSH   Screen Play by Walter Doniger and Lewis Meltzer   PRODUCED BY
ANTHONY VEILLER

ON THE WAY!   CAPTAIN HORATIO HORNBLOWER
IN COLOR BY TECHNICOLOR   *and!*   A STREETCAR NAMED DESIRE

THE TIN STAR

...the story of the ex-sheriff who'd worn it—till he'd faced one gun too many...the young sheriff he had to teach to wear it – or watch die...and the boy who lived only to wear one of his own!

THE TIN STAR

...and $40 a month – that's what they gave you for protecting people who ran like rabbits when the going got rough!

THE TIN STAR

...another superbly powerful triumph from Perlberg and Seaton, producers of "The Country Girl" and "The Proud and Profane!"

VISTAVISION ®

Paramount presents

HENRY **FONDA** · ANTHONY **PERKINS**

IN A PERLBERG·SEATON PRODUCTION

THE TIN STAR

co-starring

BETSY PALMER·MICHEL RAY

NEVILLE BRAND · JOHN McINTIRE

Produced by William Perlberg and George Seaton
Directed by Anthony Mann · Screenplay by Dudley Nichols
From a Story by Barney Slater and Joel Kane · A Paramount Release

he had to find her...
he had to find her...

THE BIGGEST, ROUGHEST, TOUGHEST... AND MOST BEAUTIFUL PICTURE EVER MADE!

WARNER BROS. PRESENT
THE C.V. WHITNEY PICTURE STARRING

JOHN WAYNE
"THE SEARCHERS"

THE STORY THAT SWEEPS
FROM THE GREAT SOUTHWEST
TO THE CANADIAN BORDER IN

VistaVision
MOTION PICTURE · HIGH FIDELITY
AND COLOR BY
TECHNICOLOR

CO-STARRING **JEFFREY HUNTER · VERA MILES**
WARD BOND · NATALIE WOOD
SCREEN PLAY BY **FRANK S. NUGENT** · EXECUTIVE PRODUCER **MERIAN C. COOPER** · ASSOCIATE PRODUCER **PATRICK FORD**

DIRECTED BY
4-TIME ACADEMY AWARD WINNER
JOHN FORD
PRESENTED BY WARNER BROS.

Musical

In the early 1930s, following the advent of sound, the movie musical became one of the most popular forms of screen fare. The early ads proclaimed "All Singing! All Dancing! All Talking!" For a while, that was enough, and in their own naive way, these early musicals were good movies. But as the use of the sound camera developed in sophistication, so did the musicals which Hollywood produced. Perhaps the plots remained naive, but the visuals were remarkable. Busby Berkeley, working primarily at Warner Bros. studio, created a series of musicals which exist today as monuments to fantasy and spectacle, and which contained a lot of wonderful music as well.

The real heyday of the movie musical, however, came in the 1940s and early 1950s, in the films created by the Arthur Freed unit at M-G-M. These were movies populated by incredibly talented performers, presented in vibrant, lavish settings. Most of them were hugely successful with the public as well. But all that changed in the 1960s and 1970s. Perhaps there were no film-makers with the creative vision of Berkeley or Freed. Perhaps the particular kind of fantasy which allowed people to break into song and to dance on crowded streets had no place in a world which was enmeshed in conflicts of stark hate and self-loathing. Contemporary musicals seldom allow for fantasy, their songs are delivered in context; they are decidedly earthbound.

A typical example of this new approach to the musical medium is the vastly overrated *All that Jazz* (1980). It is a bleak, hateful, tasteless movie in which fantasy exists only in the subconscious of the main character. In the traditional sense it is not really a musical, although it does contain a few instances of people singing and dancing of sorts. The ad for the film simply presents the title in marquee lights against a dark background—stark, just like the film.

Certainly there is a world of difference between *All That Jazz* and *Holiday Inn,* the 1942 film that introduced "Easter Parade" and "White Christmas." It was an Irving Berlin musical all the way, with the composer at the top of his form. The movie ad for *Holiday Inn* is very busy, but then it had a lot to sell—lots of new songs, two top musical performers, and even a "story" about two friends who set out to make a success of a country inn.

Stormy Weather (1943) also had a lot to offer, and the ad for it tries to show it all. The film had an all-black cast, and its audience extended well beyond any color line. The movie boasted Lena Horne, beautiful and sultry, Bill Robinson, playing himself (the story was *very* loosely based on Robinson's long career in the vaudeville theater), and Cab Calloway and Fats Waller, just playing their music and being themselves. The plot was minimal and slightly absurd, but it didn't matter: as the ad stated, the movie had "rhythm, song, and romance," and with such a cast, that was all that mattered.

Doris Day's career was just hitting its stride in 1951, and *Lullaby of Broadway* was purely a vehicle for her talents. The ad was appropriate for the film, being totally nonspecific, but promising music, songs, dancing, and Miss Day. It was a film produced with no special care, but simply meant to satisfy those who wanted to see their favorite musical star.

Annie Get Your Gun, released the previous year, was primarily Betty Hutton's show (although Howard Keel had a strong supporting role), but it was the fame of the play on which the movie was based that was the principal drawing card for audiences. Irving Berlin had written the score of wonderful songs which, along with the strong presence of Ethel Merman, gave the play a long run on Broadway. The ad for the movie was essentially selling the association with the play, although Miss Hutton was considered enough of a plus to be given a major space in the layout. This was one of the musical films produced by Arthur Freed and was done with his typical loving care.

Freed also produced *Kismet* (1955), once again a film based on a successful Broadway musical. This time Howard Keel was starred along with Ann Blyth. The ad for the film featured hordes of lovely women dressed in diaphanous harem pants. It was a very busy piece of print work, perhaps essentially so because except for its association with the hit play it was a tough sell. The film was only moderately successful, both artistically and at the box office.

Gigi, winner of the Academy Award for best picture in 1958, is considered by many to be the crowning achievement of Freed's career. Its principal distinction was that it could boast music and lyrics by Lerner and Loewe, the team who had just scored a major success on Broadway with *My Fair Lady,* and it was appropriate that it was the songs that were featured most prominently in the ad. While the cast of *Gigi* was wonderful, it contained no stars of any particular appeal. It was the overall quality of Freed's production that made it such a success.

Freed was not involved with another of M-G-M's more successful musicals, *Seven Brides for Seven Brothers,* but he might well have been. It was an exciting movie, with a crop of fresh young performers, an exceptional score of original songs, and absolutely brilliant choreography by Michael Kidd. It was a musical unique in its concept, and totally successful. It was nominated for an Academy Award as best picture for 1954,

and, while it did not win, it certainly won at the box office. The ad for the movie was fun and successful in conveying a sense of the excitement and enjoyment in store for the moviegoer.

Carousel (1956) was adapted to the big screen from the long-running Rodgers and Hammerstein musical, but something was lost in the transition. The ad included here is perhaps indicative of the problem: in most respects, what is being advertised is not the movie so much as the new Cinemascope 55 process in which it was filmed. *Carousel* suffered from a case of over-production; the moviemakers weren't content just to bring a big musical to the screen, they had to make it bigger than big. The light, affectionate touch necessary to make musicals work on the screen was missing.

Damn Yankees (1958) was another Broadway-to-Hollywood musical. In some respects it, too, was over-produced, but it was much closer to the feel of the original play than *Carousel* had been. *Yankees* was brought to the screen fresh from its stage success; it boasted a major Broadway star in the presence of Gwen Verdon; it contained more than its share of memorable and recognizable tunes. To add a touch of sex appeal, Tab Hunter was featured, and mis-casted, as the hero. All these aspects are featured prominently in the ad for the film, but none of them were enough to make the movie a major success.

Perhaps the contemporary movie-going public has lost its collective ability to suspend disbelief. There isn't the least touch of reality in a story about a man selling his soul to the devil just so the Yankees will not win the penant, especially when all the baseball players are dancing and singing from base to base. The only kind of fantasy that seems to be popular today is founded in the supernatural (and is anyone absolutely *sure* that such phenomena are not, in fact, possible?) and in science fiction—and we all know that what was science fiction a half century ago is largely fact today. But musicals should not be counted out; they are still immensely popular on television, and in time should enjoy a renaissance.

Exotic Potion at the Pool of Love... Beauties entice a man with the delectable temptation of "Rajahlakum"!

Kismet

M-G-M presents its spectacular CINEMASCOPE and COLOR production of the Broadway extravaganza!

...ecstasy of song, spectacle and love!

GREAT LOVE SONGS!

"Stranger In Paradise"

"Baubles, Bangles And Beads"

"This Is My Beloved"

and more!

AVAILABLE IN M-G-M RECORDS ALBUM

The Oasis of Delightful Imaginings... A garden paradise where lovers may dally forever drinking deeply of the joys of love!

STARRING

HOWARD KEEL
ANN BLYTH
DOLORES GRAY
VIC DAMONE

WITH
MONTY WOOLLEY · SEBASTIAN CABOT

The Secret Wall of the Wazir's Harem... Strange device that permits an intimate peek and innocent pleasure!

SCREEN PLAY BY
CHARLES LEDERER AND LUTHER DAVIS · CHARLES LEDERER AND LUTHER DAVIS
Adapted from the Musical Play "KISMET"

BOOK BY

Founded on "KISMET" by Edward Knoblock

MUSIC AND LYRICS BY
ROBERT WRIGHT AND GEORGE FORREST · Music Adapted from Themes of ALEXANDER BORODIN

PHOTOGRAPHED IN EASTMAN COLOR

DIRECTED BY
VINCENTE MINNELLI

PRODUCED BY
ARTHUR FREED

The first
Lerner-Loewe Musical
since
"My Fair Lady"
is on the screen!

GiGi

M-G-M Presents
AN ARTHUR FREED PRODUCTION
Starring
LESLIE CARON
MAURICE CHEVALIER
LOUIS JOURDAN
HERMIONE GINGOLD · EVA GABOR
JACQUES BERGERAC · ISABEL JEANS
Screen Play and Lyrics by **ALAN JAY LERNER** · Music by **FREDERICK LOEWE**
Based on the Novel by **COLETTE** · Costumes, Scenery & Production Design by **CECIL BEATON** · In CinemaScope And METROCOLOR
Directed by **VINCENTE MINNELLI**

"Thank Heaven For Little Girls"

"She's Not Thinking Of Me!"

"The Parisians"

"Gigi"

"I'm Glad I'm Not Young Anymore"

"The Night They Invented Champagne"

Hear the LERNER-LOEWE Score now available in the new MGM RECORDS Sound Track Album

ROY SCHEIDER

All that work.
All that glitter.
All that pain.
All that love.
All that crazy
rhythm.
All that jazz.

TWENTIETH CENTURY-FOX & COLUMBIA PICTURES PRESENT IN A

ROY SCHEIDER BOB FOSSE FILM ALL THAT JAZZ

ALSO STARRING   SPECIAL GUEST APPEARANCES

JESSICA LANGE ANN REINKING LELAND PALMER CLIFF GORMAN & BEN VEREEN

DIRECTOR OF PHOTOGRAPHY   EDITOR   PRODUCTION DESIGNER   FANTASY DESIGNER   MUSIC SUPERVISOR & CONDUCTOR
GIUSEPPE ROTUNNO   ALAN HEIM   PHILIP ROSENBERG   TONY WALTON   RALPH BURNS

EXECUTIVE   PRODUCED   ASSOCIATE   KENNETH UTT & WOLFGANG GLATTES
PRODUCERS DANIEL MELNICK   BY   ROBERT ALAN AURTHUR   PRODUCERS
COLOR BY TECHNICOLOR®   NOW IN PAPERBACK FROM JOVE
© 1979 TWENTIETH CENTURY-FOX AND COLUMBIA PICTURES INDUSTRIES INC.

DIRECTED   WRITTEN
BY BOB FOSSE   BY ROBERT ALAN AURTHUR AND BOB FOSSE

R RESTRICTED
UNDER 17 REQUIRES ACCOMPANYING
PARENT OR ADULT GUARDIAN

Romance

Nearly all movies contain an element of romance, but some are primarily romances, their stories revolving around the romantic involvements of two—and often more—people. Few films are purely romance, however; usually they overlap with one of the other principal genres such as comedy or musicals.

However, some films do exist solely as romances. *The Enchanted Cottage* was the story of two people whose love erased all handicaps. *Wuthering Heights,* one of the best films ever made, was a classic story of love triumphant. *Love Story* was just what the title implied, and it was from that movie that one of the most famous ad lines was derived: "Love is never having to say you're sorry." Most romantic films are sold primarily on the strength of the featured star or stars, although identification with a famous novel is a frequent plus.

Moulin Rouge (1934) was billed as a "romance with music." It starred Constance Bennett at the height of her career, playing a dual role. It was not an especially significant film, but it was very stylish—as was the ad, which reflected the mode of the time. Perhaps the most notable aspect of the film was that Miss Bennett, never known as a singer, introduced the now-famous torch song, "Boulevard of Broken Dreams."

According to the ad line for *Til We Meet Again* (1939), "You'll LIVE this Romance." It starred Merle Oberon and George Brent, and they were the principal selling point for the film. The copy approach was totally nonspecific, telling nothing of the plot (even the visuals offered no clues, except for a drawing of an ocean liner, where most of the action took place), merely promising the moviegoer "a *really* thrilling romance."

The war in Europe was the background for the 1942 romantic film, *This Above All,* based on Eric Knight's best-selling novel. The movie was technically a war drama, but the love story was paramount, and certainly the two popular stars—Tyrone Power and Joan Fontaine—were powerful romantic figures.

The pairing of Lana Turner and Spencer Tracy as a romantic team seems a little unusual perhaps. He was known for his dramatic roles and for the "real guy" involvement he brought to all the parts he played. Lana Turner was a sultry vamp, often unsympathetic in her earthy characterizations of hard-hearted women, a little shy on class. Despite the claims made by the ad, *Cass Timberlane* (1947) was *not* one of Sinclair Lewis' greatest novels, but it did translate into a popular movie. The ad promised these two stars in a dramatic love story. In fact, the on-screen chemistry between the two stars worked very well, and it *was* an M-G-M movie (which always meant that it would be a production with some class), so few who paid their money were disappointed.

Like *Til We Meet Again, Body and Soul* (1947) employed ads which told virtually nothing of the movie's plot, relying instead on the appeal of the stars—and, in *Body and Soul,* a strong suggestion of sex—to lure people to the theaters. John Garfield had tremendous sex appeal for an awful lot of women; as the ad stated, he was "a guy that women go for." For the men, there was the leggy lady seen draped over the "o" in *Body.* Hazel Brooks, introduced in this film, was hardly heard from again. Whatever the ad was selling, the chemistry worked—the movie was a major box office success.

Lana Turner movies were almost a category unto themselves. Invariably they were romantic, many of them were "tear-jerkers," most of them were successful—but not all of them. *A Life of Her Own* (1950) was *not* one of her successes, although it had all the elements. As the ad copy declared, Lana portrayed a young woman from Kansas who took New York by storm, becoming a famous fashion model. The plot allowed for big city glamour, for beautiful clothes (a staple in Lana Turner movies), and for extensive romantic involvements, but that "something extra" was missing, that element which could have extended the audience for the film beyond the star's legion of loyal fans.

Roman Holiday was a major success for everyone involved. Set in Rome—a perfect city for romantic adventures, it offered a wonderful story of a young princess who escapes the demands or confines of her position for one romantic day with a handsome American reporter. But, most of all, it introduced Audery Hepburn to American audiences, and she proved to be every bit as "exciting" as the ad promised. It was an auspicious beginning for her career—the role won her the Academy Award for best actress in 1953. The powers behind the scenes who decided to go with the unknown actress were taking a great gamble, but they played it well, featuring her name above the title (but below that of co-star Gregory Peck) and directing the main ad copy to highlight her presence. It may have been a gamble, but it certainly paid off.

One of the most successful films of 1955 was *Love Is a Many-Splendored Thing.* It was based on a best-selling novel and starred two very popular performers, William Holden and Jennifer Jones, both of whom were given major play in the ad. However, what distinguished the film and made it such a success was the story dealing with the semi-taboo subject of love between two races, a subject which the ad copy played up extensively. Another key element to the success of the film, not mentioned in the ad, was the phenomenally popular title song which hit the top of the music charts and stayed there for months.

Despite the presence of two very appealing young actors—Audrey Hepburn and Anthony Perkins, *Green Mansions* was a major failure. Perhaps it was the lack of chemistry between the two stars that caused it to disappoint their fans. Or maybe it was the extreme softness of the novel by W. H. Hudson on which the movie was based. Whatever the reason, audiences in 1959 simply were not waiting for a love story about Rima, "the girl of the virgin forest," and Abel, the first man to love her. Perhaps sensing it had a major disaster on its hands, M-G-M must have instructed its ad men to sell everything in sight. While prominently featuring the two principals in a decidedly non-passionate embrace, the copy proceeded to exclaim over "menace . . . amid the orchids!", the fact that *Reader's Digest* had condensed the book (!), that cameras had been sent to the Amazon jungles "for 'on location' thrills!", and that the movie contained "marvelous music" by Villa-Lobos and "tribal dancers" created by Katherine Dunham. No one was impressed, and virtually no one saw the movie.

Love stories had come a long way by 1978. Strict codes which had prescribed exactly what could and could not be shown on the screen had been thrown out the window, leaving filmmakers to their own discretion as to just how graphically they might depict the love two characters felt for each other. Despite what its "R" rating might imply, *Coming Home* was a discreet, tasteful film which dealt with a difficult and different kind of love story. In some respects, it might be classified as a war film, since it dealt with what war does to men's bodies and minds, and to the women who love them. The ad for the film pictured the three principals and indicated through their positioning that there was a kind of triangle involved. The movie was deservedly popular, earning Academy Awards for best actor and actress for John Voight and Jane Fonda respectively.

Whatever the decade, there is a market for romance. As with *Coming Home,* it may be tempered with a heavy dose of reality, but it remains romance nonetheless. It is the kind of film that gives hope to the loveless and unhappy. There is, in fact, an increasing trend toward romantic movies, and they seem to be enjoying greater box office success.

YOU'LL SEE TWO CONSTANCE BENNETTS...

in this intoxicating, spectacular romance with music! ...the Connie you've always loved—blonde and enticing...And a new Connie—brunette, seductive and ravishing! ... teamed with Franchot Tone to create "the perfect lovers" of the screen!

JOSEPH M. SCHENCK
Presents
CONSTANCE
BENNETT

MOULIN ROUGE

FRANCHOT TONE

TULLIO CARMINATI
RUSS COLUMBO
BOSWELL SISTERS
Directed by Sidney Lanfield

20th
CENTURY
PICTURE

A DARRYL F. ZANUCK Production...Released thru UNITED ARTISTS

She was Han Suyin, the fascinating Eurasian...
He was Mark Elliot, the American correspondent...

*A love
that defied
5000 years
of tradition!*

The price they pay when they come out of their secret garden
and face the world in modern-day Hong Kong—makes this
one of the screen's unforgettable experiences.

*20th Century-Fox captures all the beauty and rapture of
Han Suyin's true best-seller.*

WILLIAM HOLDEN · JENNIFER JONES
Love is a Many-Splendored Thing

with TORIN
THATCHER **CinemaScope** COLOR by
DE LUXE

PRODUCED BY | DIRECTED BY | SCREEN PLAY BY
BUDDY ADLER · HENRY KING · JOHN PATRICK

One of the greatest novels Sinclair Lewis ever wrote...now becomes one of the screen's most dramatic love stories from M-G-M

SPENCER TRACY · LANA TURNER
ZACHARY SCOTT

Cass Timberlane

TOM DRAKE · MARY ASTOR · ALBERT DEKKER

Screen Play by DONALD OGDEN STEWART · Adaptation by DONALD OGDEN STEWART and SONYA LEVIEN
Based on the Novel by SINCLAIR LEWIS
Directed by GEORGE SIDNEY · Produced by ARTHUR HORNBLOW, JR.
A METRO-GOLDWYN-MAYER PICTURE

"THE KIND OF CHEMISTRY TO START LINING UP

A Jerome Hellman Production
A Hal Ashby Film

Jane Fonda
Jon Voight *Bruce Dern*
in
"Coming Home"

Screenplay by **Waldo Salt** and **Robert C. Jones** Story by **Nancy Dowd** Director of Photography **Haskell Wexler**
Associate Producer **Bruce Gilbert** Produced by **Jerome Hellman** Directed by **Hal Ashby**

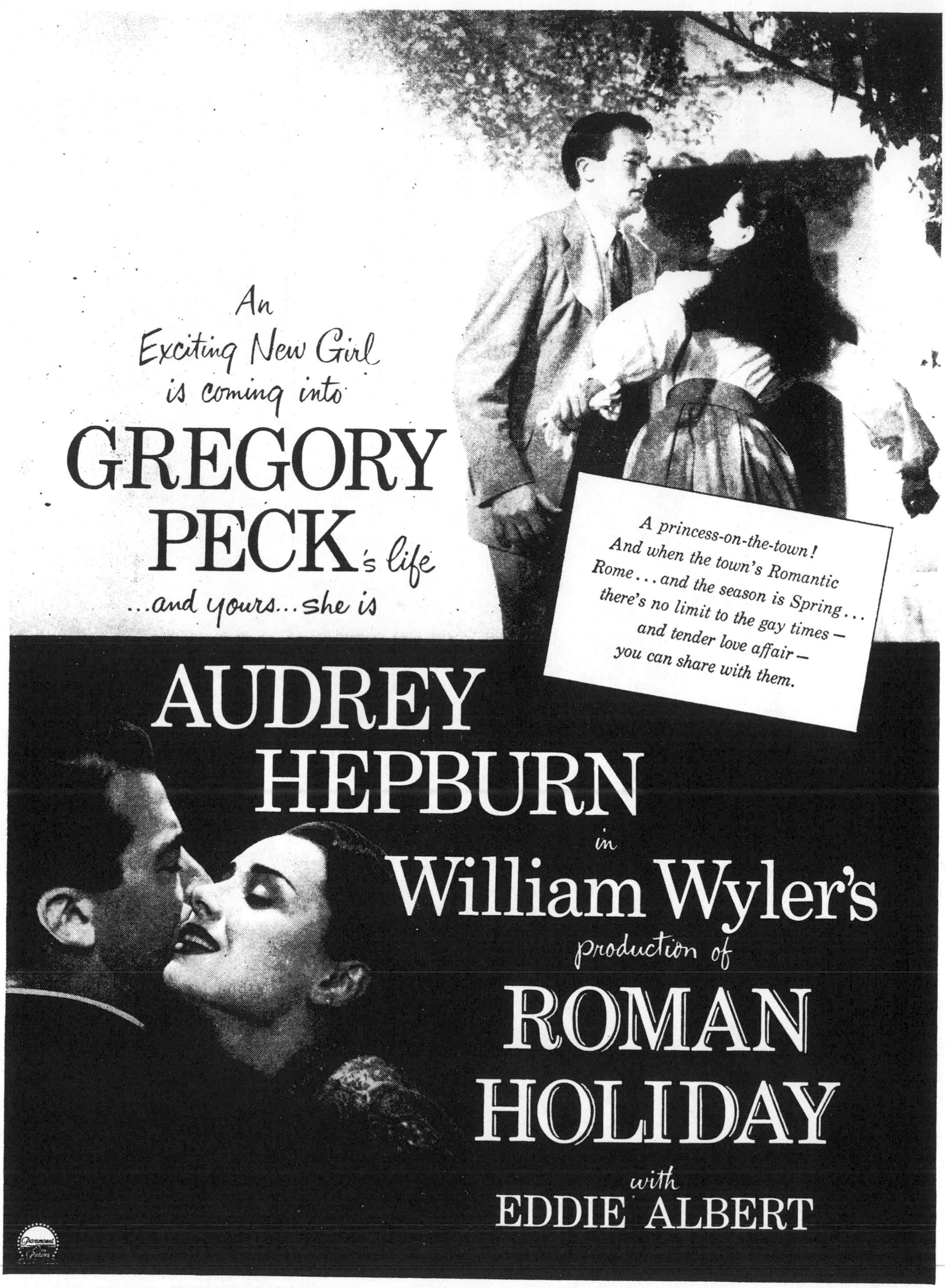

An Exciting New Girl is coming into **GREGORY PECK**'s life ...and yours... she is

A princess-on-the-town! And when the town's Romantic Rome... and the season is Spring... there's no limit to the gay times — and tender love affair — you can share with them.

AUDREY HEPBURN

in William Wyler's production of

ROMAN HOLIDAY

with **EDDIE ALBERT**

Produced & Directed by WILLIAM WYLER · Screenplay by IAN McLELLAN HUNTER & JOHN DIGHTON
Story by Ian McLellan Hunter · A PARAMOUNT PICTURE

128

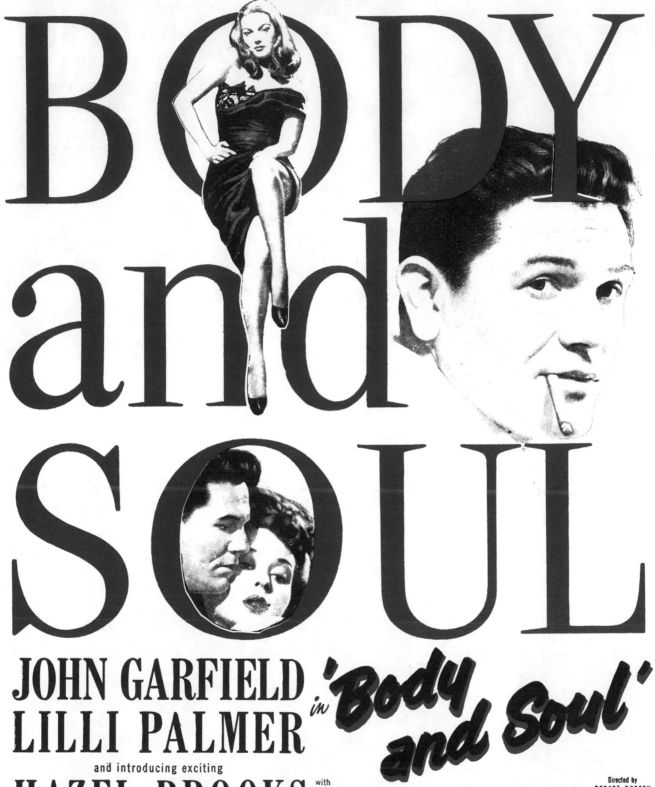

The story of a guy that women go for!

BODY and SOUL

JOHN GARFIELD
LILLI PALMER in 'Body and Soul'

and introducing exciting
HAZEL BROOKS with **ANNE REVERE**
as ALICE

WILLIAM CONRAD · JOSEPH PEVNEY
LLOYD GOFF · CANADA LEE
Original screenplay by ABRAHAM POLONSKY
RELEASED THRU UNITED ARTISTS

Directed by
ROBERT ROSSEN
Produced by
BOB ROBERTS

A new climax in entertainment from **THE ENTERPRISE STUDIOS**

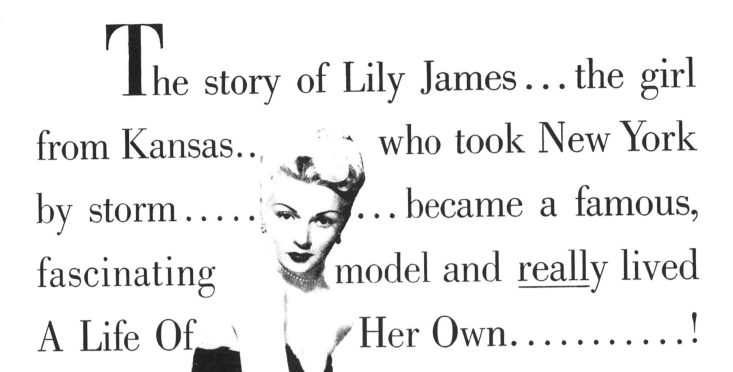

The story of Lily James…the girl from Kansas… who took New York by storm…… …became a famous, fascinating model and really lived A Life Of Her Own…………!

There were many men in her life … but with him she knew love— and its heartbreak!…

M-G-M presents

LANA TURNER

RAY MILLAND

in

"A Life Of Her Own"

TOM EWELL · LOUIS CALHERN
ANN DVORAK · BARRY SULLIVAN
MARGARET PHILLIPS
JEAN HAGEN

Written by ISOBEL LENNART
Directed by   Produced by
GEORGE CUKOR · VOLDEMAR VETLUGUIN
A METRO-GOLDWYN-MAYER PICTURE

OUT OF THE BOOK . . .
ON TO THE SCREEN!

Flaming into your hearts
with all its dramatic fervor—

The emotional thrills, the action-jammed dynamite make a great book into an even greater picture!

Tyrone
POWER · FONTAINE
Joan

DARRYL F. ZANUCK'S production

THIS ABOVE ALL

by ERIC KNIGHT

Directed by ANATOLE LITVAK

with
Thomas Mitchell
Henry Stephenson
Nigel Bruce · Gladys
Cooper · Philip Merivale
Sara Allgood
Alexander Knox

Screen Play by R. C. Sherriff

20th CENTURY FOX

Cops And Robbers

Cops and robber films were a mainstay of the movie business in the 1930s. Prohibition had given rise to real-life gangsters, men who fought the law and each other in an effort to control the rackets and to make them pay. As usual, Hollywood was quick to capitalize on the headlines these outlaws created. While some of the popularity for this kind of movie waned in the years following the repeal of prohibition, it nevertheless has remained continually popular as a genre of film, featuring stories which were frequently taken from the headlines of the day.

G-Men (1935) was one of the old-fashion kind of cops and robbers movies. The story was basic and uncomplicated: there were good guys on one side, and bad guys on the other. In this instance, the only complication derived from the presence of James Cagney as the star of the film. As the ad emphasized, Cagney had traditionally played the bad guy, his most famous characterization being the title role in *The Public Enemy.* It is a striking ad visually and is typical of the 1930s approach in its maximum use of copy.

Another movie in the mold of the 1930s gangster films was *The Roaring Twenties,* a 1939 actioner selling the nostalgia of violence. Once again, Jimmy Cagney was the star, but this time he was paired romantically with Priscilla Lane (of the singing Lane Sisters) who was popular for a brief time. The ad, typically busy, promised "the heyday of the hotcha"—gangsters, flappers, booze, and jazz. The movie has endured as a particular favorite of the genre.

Humphrey Bogart had received secondary billing in *The Roaring Twenties,* but two years later he was the star of *High Sierra,* playing the part of

Roy "Mad Dog" Earle. The ad for this film was particularly effective; it gave a very real sense of action, dealing with a man running from the law, trapped by his own escape. It conveys the theme of one man against the world; and then as now, audiences love to champion the underdog. The movie was very successful and remains one of the favorites of Bogart's legion of fans.

"T 'n T" stood for (Robert) Taylor and (Lana) Turner, teamed in the steamy 1942 gangland thriller, *Johnny Eager.* It was a movie with a strong romantic angle, as the ad emphasized, pairing two very attractive, sexy stars. Turner was cast as a "high-born beauty" blindly in love with Taylor, "the most icy-hearted Big Shot gangland ever knew . . . almost 100% bad." Like its stars, the ad was sexy as well; it remains a classic effort. In *Johnny Eager,* "T 'n T" indeed meant box office dynamite.

Robert Mitchum was a big, brawny man, with sleepy, "bedroom" eyes. Female fans found him very sexy, and he was at his sexiest in roles in which he was cast as a tough he-man. As a result, Mitchum spent much of his career playing in cops and robber movies. The ad for *The Big Steal* (1949) was selling Mitchum, along with the promise of action. It was essentially a man's picture, geared to a male audience, providing plenty of tough action. The film attracted a large female audience, however, due to the lure of Mitchum making love to Jane Greer. Greer was a fine actress, but she was not especially glamorous—certainly not like a Lana Turner—and women in the audience could identify with her, picturing themselves in her place.

Kirk Douglas was another actor who was very

popular with female moviegoers. He appeared tough, but there was a sense of inner tenderness about him that made women respond. In *Detective Story* (1951) he had one of the major successes of his early career. The ad for this film was selling Douglas as a popular action star, along with the movie's association with a successful Broadway play. Both Douglas and his co-star, Eleanor Parker, were nominated for Oscars for their roles, as was Lee Grant (not billed in this ad) in a sparkling supporting role.

The Enforcer was another 1951 film in the cops and robber genre. It was not especially distinguished and is memorable primarily because of the presence of Humphrey Bogart, the perennial tough guy. The ad for this film is dramatic, with bold visuals and copy that drew attention to the plot concerning a district attorney (Bogart) determined to protect a young woman who was witness to a crime that has caused her to be marked for extermination by the underworld gangs.

Humphrey Bogart also starred in the 1955 film, *The Desperate Hours* (Bogart's next-to-last movie). This time, he was on the other side of the law playing the part of a criminal who, with two cronies, intruded upon a suburban household in their escape from the law. Based on a highly successful book and play, the movie co-starred Fredric March as the head of the family terrorized by Bogart. Visually the ad told most of the story, leaving out the ending, of course. Under the guidance of master director William Wyler, the film proved a major success.

The FBI Story was a slightly different kind of cops and robber film. The "cops" in the case were FBI-men; the story detailed the career of one of these agents in particular, played by James Stewart. Because the film did span so many years, beginning in the 1920s and continuing up until 1959 (the year the film was released), there were many bad guys. It was quite episodic in structure, with the characters of Stewart and Vera Miles, who played his wife, being the connecting thread. The ad for the movie took the point of view of the wife and featured a kind of monologue by her regarding her life as the wife of an FBI-man. Visually there was nothing too compelling about the ad, but the movie succeeded on the strength of its title and the presence of Stewart as the star.

In *Dog Day Afternoon* (1975), the real hero was not one of the cops, but rather a robber—actually a very eccentric, lovable would-be robber. As the ad copy points out, the whole robbery should have taken ten minutes, but ended up being a twelve-hour media event. The film was based on a factual incident; the characters were modeled after real people. Al Pacino, an actor of an entirely different species from Bogart or Cagney, created a quirky kind of anti-hero, totally lovable and believable. The ad did much to convey the sense of the film: a little man trapped and terrified by a situation he doesn't know how to get out of. This was the kind of "little man" film that people could relate to; it was very successful.

Frank Sinatra has been a major box office draw for many years, but *The First Deadly Sin* (1980) was not one of his successes. The movie was a very downbeat film that suffered from a severe split between the action and romance elements. Essentially, it was the story of a New York City policeman and his ailing wife, played by Sinatra and Faye Dunaway respectively. The ad for the film was quite attractive. It played down the action element and featured instead the two stars over a gloomy city street. The ad effectively conveyed the gloomy spirit of the movie, which probably was not for the best—certainly not at the box office.

The Postman Always Rings Twice was another movie that failed at the box office despite great expectations and an effective ad campaign. The ad was the key approach the filmmakers used, ignoring completely the mystery/murder aspect and emphasizing the steamy sexual involvement of the two principals. This particular tact was chosen primarily because the 1946 version of the movie has succeeded largely on the strength of the on-screen chemistry between Lana Turner and John Garfield. The story in both versions was essentially the same murder mystery, but in 1981 it was decided that the sex angle would better attract an audience. As it turned out, however, the legend, "You will feel the heat," promised more than the film delivered and the audience never materialized.

TAYLOR 'N TURNER

"You're cruel, Johnnie. You're almost 100% bad. But whatever you are, darling, you're my man!"

They're *dynamite* in

JOHNNY EAGER

The flaming drama of a high-born beauty who blindly loved the most icy-hearted Big Shot gangland ever knew.

A MERVYN LeROY Production with
EDWARD ARNOLD

VAN HEFLIN · ROBERT STERLING · PATRICIA DANE
GLENDA FARRELL · HENRY O'NEILL · DIANA LEWIS

Screen Play by John Lee Mahin and James Edward Grant
A METRO-GOLDWYN-MAYER PICTURE · Directed by MERVYN LeROY
Produced by JOHN W. CONSIDINE, Jr.

Your name is Lucy Hardesty and you married a man from the FBI...

So you were often on the move. Indian murders in Oklahoma. A spy chase in New York. A killing in Chicago. You couldn't call it dull. And the fact was, your kids loved it...

You didn't celebrate when Congress passed the law that enabled your husband to carry a gun. And you didn't sleep the night he went after deadly public enemy John Dillinger — or all the other nights with all the other hoodlums...

You never got rich. You were often scared and alone. But you had something that made it all work. Something called love. And it turned out to be a wonderful life...

And now it has turned out to be a wonderful motion picture!

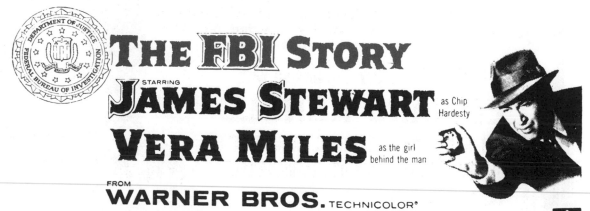

THE FBI STORY
STARRING
JAMES STEWART as Chip Hardesty
VERA MILES as the girl behind the man

FROM
WARNER BROS. TECHNICOLOR®

A MERVYN LeROY Production · Screenplay by RICHARD L. BREEN and JOHN TWIST · Directed by MERVYN LeROY · Music by MAX STEINER

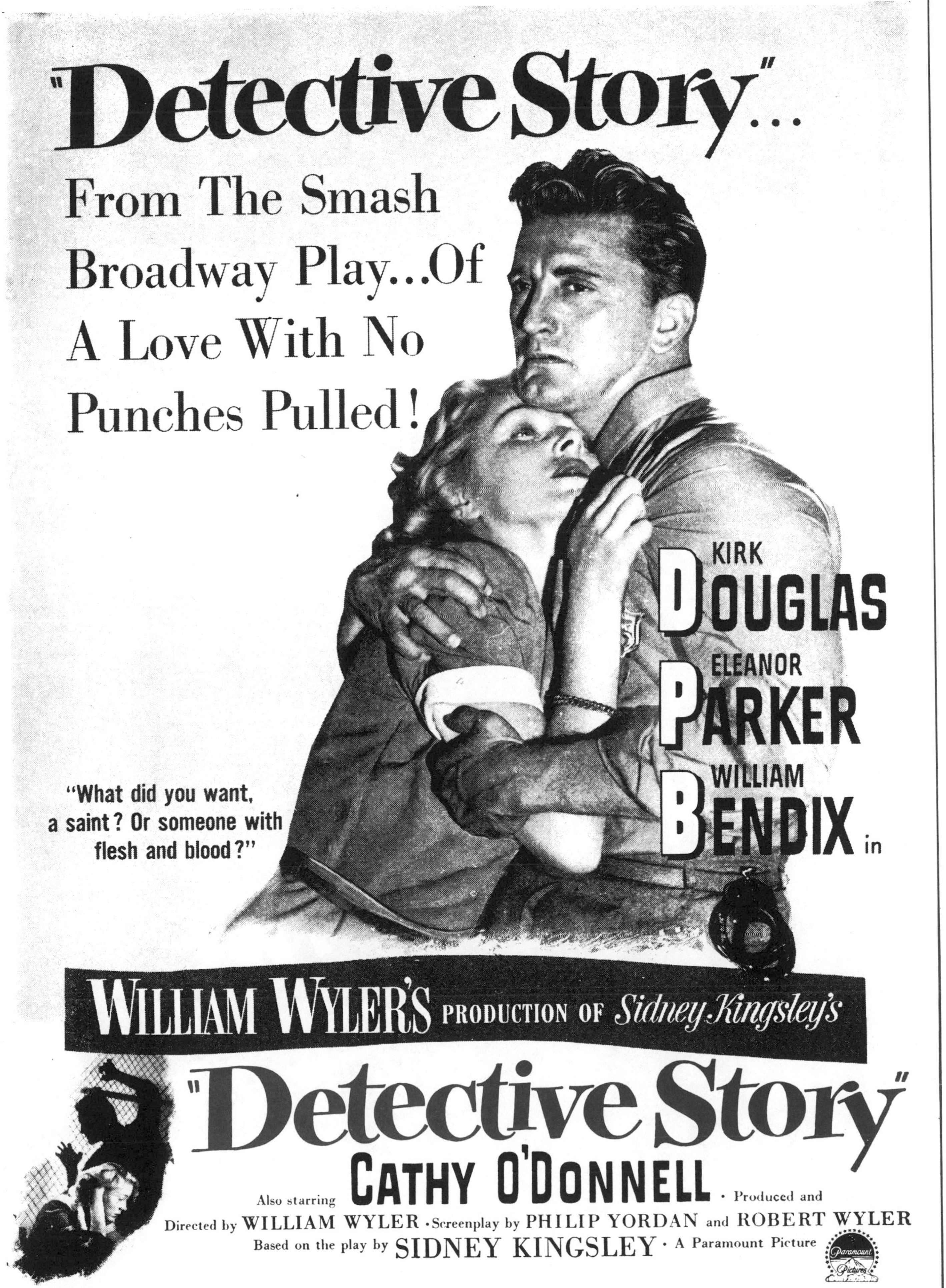

"Detective Story"...

From The Smash Broadway Play...Of A Love With No Punches Pulled!

KIRK **DOUGLAS**

ELEANOR **PARKER**

WILLIAM **BENDIX** in

"What did you want, a saint? Or someone with flesh and blood?"

WILLIAM WYLER'S PRODUCTION OF *Sidney Kingsley's*

"Detective Story"

CATHY O'DONNELL

Also starring · Produced and Directed by **WILLIAM WYLER** · Screenplay by **PHILIP YORDAN** and **ROBERT WYLER** Based on the play by **SIDNEY KINGSLEY** · A Paramount Picture

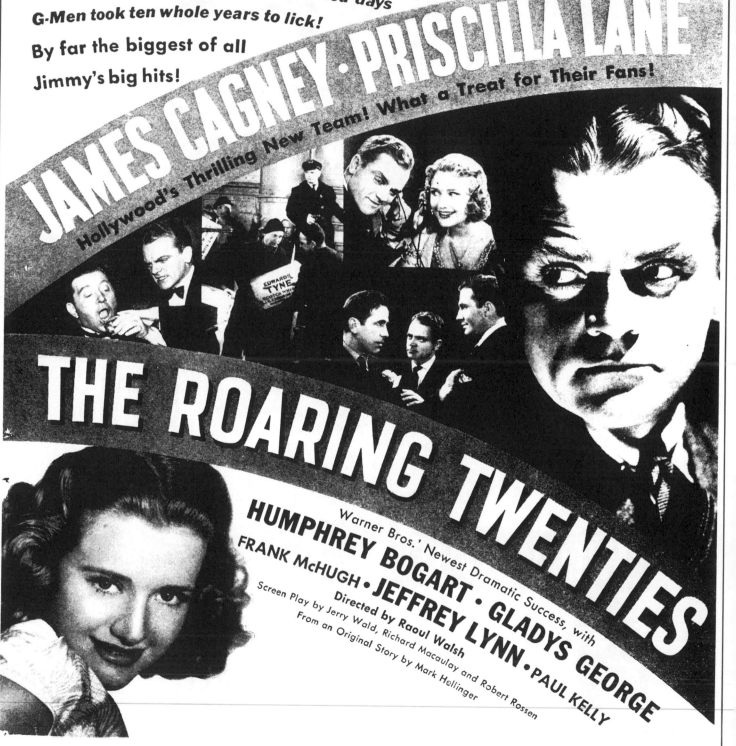

A ROARING ERA becomes A ROARING HIT!

Here's more screen excitement than ever you've seen before!
America at its maddest! America at its merriest . . .
the land of the free gone wild! It's the heyday
of the hotcha — *the shock-crammed days*
G-Men took ten whole years to lick!
By far the biggest of all
Jimmy's big hits!

JAMES CAGNEY · PRISCILLA LANE

Hollywood's Thrilling New Team! What a Treat for Their Fans!

THE ROARING TWENTIES

Warner Bros.' Newest Dramatic Success, with

HUMPHREY BOGART · GLADYS GEORGE

FRANK McHUGH · **JEFFREY LYNN** · PAUL KELLY

Screen Play by Jerry Wald, Richard Macaulay and Robert Rossen

Directed by Raoul Walsh

From an Original Story by Mark Hellinger

"Get off the streets Angela Vetto!"

IT WAS THE ENFORCER SPEAKING... THE DOUBLE-FISTED DISTRICT ATTORNEY WHO MATCHED HIMSELF AGAINST A NATION-WIDE EMPIRE OF "KILLERS-FOR-HIRE". THIS WAS HIS CRUCIAL MOMENT—— THE ONE LAST THING——TO SAVE THE SINGLE LIVING WITNESS THE UNDERWORLD WAS SWORN TO GET!

THE MOST VICIOUS WORDS IN CRIMEDOM and Angela learned them all!

'CONTRACT': an order for a killing
'HIT': a murder victim
'TROOP': the local murder mob
'FINGER': he sets up the 'hit'

The real hero of this story is not Humphrey Bogart... it is every fighting District Attorney in the land!

HUMPHREY

BOGART AS

"THE ENFORCER"

PRESENTED BY WARNER BROS.

WITH ZERO MOSTEL • TED de CORSIA • ROY ROBERTS • EVERETT SLOANE • WRITTEN BY MARTIN RACKIN

DIRECTED BY
BRETAIGNE WINDUST • MILTON SPERLING • UNITED STATES PICTURES PROD • WARNER BROS.
PRODUCED BY   DISTRIBUTED BY

MITCHUM... IN HIS NEWEST PICTURE!

It's a tough, terrific adventure in grand larceny that gets him deep into the wilds of Mexico...and deeper in love and danger with **GORGEOUS JANE GREER** on the trail of a fortune in hot money!

RKO PRESENTS

ROBERT MITCHUM
JANE GREER · WILLIAM BENDIX
in
THE BIG STEAL

with

PATRIC KNOWLES · RAMON NOVARRO · DON ALVARADO · JOHN QUALEN

Executive Producer SID ROGELL · Produced by JACK J. GROSS · Directed by DON SIEGEL

Screen Play by GEOFFREY HOMES and GERALD DRAYSON ADAMS

Based on the famous Saturday Evening Post Story "The Road to Carmichael's" by RICHARD WORMSER

RKO RADIO PICTURES

"The picture to beat for the next set of Oscars."
—Gary Arnold
WASHINGTON POST

The robbery should have taken 10 minutes. 4 hours later, the bank was like a circus sideshow. 8 hours later, it was the hottest thing on live T. V. 12 hours later, it was all history. And it's all true.

AL PACINO in DOG DAY AFTERNOON

Also Starring
An Artists Entertainment Complex Inc Production

R RESTRICTED Under 17 requires accompanying Parent or Adult Guardian

JOHN CAZALE · JAMES BRODERICK and CHARLES DURNING as Moretti · Screenplay by FRANK PIERSON · Produced by MARTIN BREGMAN and MARTIN ELFAND · Directed by SIDNEY LUMET · Film Editor DEDE ALLEN · TECHNICOLOR® From Warner Bros ⓦ A Warner Communications Company

OPENS CHRISTMAS DAY AT A THEATRE NEAR YOUR HOME

He's searching for a killer.

She's searching for a miracle.

...and time
is running out.

FRANK
SINATRA

FAYE
DUNAWAY

THE
FIRST
DEADLY SIN

ELLIOTT KASTNER PRESENTS AN ARTANIS-CINEMA VII PRODUCTION
STARRING JAMES WHITMORE   DAVID DUKES
BRENDA VACCARO   MARTIN GABEL AND ANTHONY ZERBE
DIRECTED BY BRIAN HUTTON SCREENPLAY BY MANN RUBIN FROM THE NOVEL BY LAWRENCE SANDERS
MUSIC BY GORDON JENKINS PRODUCED BY GEORGE PAPPAS & MARK SHANKER
EXECUTIVE PRODUCERS FRANK SINATRA & ELLIOTT KASTNER
COLOR BY MOVIELAB   CAMERA EQUIPMENT BY PANAFLEX   RELEASED BY FILMWAYS PICTURES
COPYRIGHT FIRST DEADLY SIN COMPANY MCMLXXX ALL RIGHTS RESERVED

You will feel the heat.

JACK NICHOLSON
JESSICA LANGE

IN A BOB RAFELSON FILM

the POSTMAN ALWAYS Rings Twice

NOW PLAYING New York, Los Angeles, Chicago, Toronto · National Release Begins April 3rd.

Comedy

Hollywood may have abandoned Westerns and musicals for the time being. Science fiction may have become big box office, employing incredible space "hardware" and gadgetry. Drama may have become more and more realistic. But comedy has simply gone on and on, whether it be slapstick, social comedy, comedy of manners, parody, satire, romance, or whatever.

In the early days of Hollywood, most comedy was very broad, usually of the slapstick variety. During the 1930s it became generally more sophisticated, introducing a distinct and witty element of sex. It was in that period that the screwball comedy came into vogue. The 1940s were, of course, war years, and while broad, farcical comedy was still popular, there was a strong movement toward social comedy, laughter with a touch of parody, sometimes sharp, often turned inward. During the 1950s, the comedies were frequently zany, sometimes with a kind of leering, sexual innuendo. The 1960s reflected a trend toward black humor. By the 1970s, Hollywood was starting to repeat itself, taking old forms of humor and adapting them for a new generation of moviegoers. These comedies were sometimes zany, sometimes screwball, often black in tone, usually sexual, frequently social commentaries, and just about always slapstick.

Nine to Five (1980) was not especially popular with the critics, but it scored big at the box office. Much of the success must be credited to the presence of three big stars, all major attractions. Another major element, however, was the theme—getting even with the boss by showing him just how the place really should operate. The approach was a kind of amalgam of farce and slapstick, with a heavy touch of fantasy. The ad told the story, fairly well, although given all the pre-release publicity attending the film, it probably would have been just as big a success had the ad run only the title and the names of the three stars.

Forty years earlier, Katharine Hepburn's career had been given a second life through the success of *The Philadelphia Story* (two years earlier, theater owners had named her "box office poison"). The movie was based on a popular Broadway play which had, in fact, been tailor-made to suit Miss Hepburn's talents. Taking no chances, however, M-G-M co-starred her with two very popular leading men, Cary Grant and James Stewart. The ad for the movie included here is one of the cleverest ever, giving enough of the plot to entice, while interspersing cartoon sketches to convey the kind of cockeyed humor which distinguished this film. The movie was a major success for all concerned, and was remade in 1956 as a musical, this time titled *High Society.*

Born Yesterday (1950) marked the high point of the tragically brief career of the wonderful comedienne Judy Holliday. The ad for this film was both clever and prophetic: Miss Holliday had only one starring movie role to her credit prior to this one *(Adam's Rib),* yet she was given maximum play in the ad, with the copy proclaiming that "After you've seen 'Born Yesterday,' your favorite new star will be Judy Holliday." The studio was obviously banking on the popular reaction to this film and its star to attract a wider audience through word-of-mouth. The tactic worked: audiences loved it and so did the critics, and the role of Billie Dawn won Miss Holliday an Academy Award as best actress of the year.

The Lady Eve (1941) was a creation of the genius of Preston Sturges, a director who made a series of highly successful social comedies which affectionately parodied various aspects of American life. The ad for this movie took a semi-cartoon approach in presenting the two popular stars, Barbara Stanwyck and Henry Fonda, hinting only vaguely at a plot involving a woman's use of her feminine wiles to get her man. It is interesting to note just how prominently Mr. Sturges is featured in this ad, an unusual approach in most comedy films.

Although the ad men had no way of knowing it at the time, *Teacher's Pet* (1958) marked a departure in the career of Doris Day that was to prove to be very successful. Up to this point in her career, she had been featured in mild suspense/thriller films, as well as basically plotless musical vehicles. With *Teacher's Pet* she began a series of very popular comedies which continued over the next ten years. The ad for this film is particularly clever, utilizing various classroom subjects as taking-off points for scenes from the movie, relying heavily on sexual innuendo. Although Clark Gable was given first billing (his fourth-from-last film), it was really Miss Day's day.

Life With Father (1947) brought to the screen the phenomenally successful Broadway play [as the ad copy said: "Welcome! The longest-run stage hit in history *(8 straight years!)* is a Warner Picture now!], and that was what the ad men were selling. The ad itself was very smart, conveying a sense of fun and comedy, featuring a picture of the family midst a cartoon landscape. The stars of the film, William Powell and Irene Dunne, were given major space in the ad despite the fact that at that point in their careers neither was any longer a box office draw. It really didn't matter; this was a movie which sold entirely on its title.

The copy used in the ad for *The Ghost and Mrs. Muir (1947)* refers to a "sly smile," and "sly" was the approach the ad took to promote this strange movie. Basically the film tells the story of a woman who falls in love with the ghost of a sea captain—by all indications, a "tough sell." The movie was popular, however, despite this seemingly unlikely combination of the supernatural with comedy and romance. Perhaps the ad hit the right tone with its vague allusions to "a haunting kiss," and to a "man-woman affair like

nothing on earth." It also wisely played up its two attractive and appealing stars, Gene Tierney and Rex Harrison.

My Man Godfrey had been an extremely successful movie in 1936, starring Carole Lombard and William Powell, and it remains a wonderful example of "screwball" comedy at its best. Remade twenty-one years later, starring June Allyson and David Niven, it was a bomb. The chemistry that had worked so well between Lombard and Powell simply wasn't there with Allyson and Niven. What had been screwball was turned into something insipid and tedious. Given these bleak realities, the ad men did a yeoman's job of creating an appealing ad, showing a disconcerted Niven in various compromising situations, all of it relying heavily on hints of sex: "She wanted breakfast in bed . . . but she didn't want to eat alone!!!" Despite the extra exclamation points, the film was a major failure.

The team of Bob Hope, Bing Crosby, and Dorothy Lamour made a string of "Road" pictures in the 1940s (there was a final one in the 1950s, *Road to Bali*). *Road to Utopia* (1945) was the fourth in this series, and easily one of the best. The ad assumes a familiarity with these other movies *("zanier* than *Zanzibar"),* and a built-in audience affection for these stars. An especially clever note in the ad comes in the picturing of Miss Lamour in her inevitable sarong while burying her hands in a fur muff, since *Utopia* placed much of its action in the frozen north. It was a zany ad for a very funny movie.

Stir Crazy (1980) was a major box office hit, despite the fact that it was fried by the critics. The ad for the movie is interesting since it managed to take a minor element in the film—Gene Wilder and Richard Pryor dressed in bird costumes—and turn it into a metaphor with which to outline the entire plot of the movie. It was an arresting image, however, and highly successful in identifying the film as a crazy, implausible, hilarious piece of work.

Laughter is a universal emotion, a sign of sanity in the face of madness. Comedies will remain popular—they may get blacker, they may get crazier, but they will endure, serving as a kind of antedote to some of the bizarre realities of everyday life. Whether they feature madcap blondes, eccentric millionaires, or bumbling cops, comedy films speak a language we all understand.

Once upon a cockeyed time...

there was a ravishing redhead who was very, very elegant and fancied herself as a kind of goddess. *(Imagine!)*... And she was all set to marry a truly stuffy guy ...when her ex-husband showed up. Now *he* was a regular fellow with many human frailties such as and and you-know-what. This time he brought with him a handsome reporter with candid camera and candid girl friend by means of which he hoped to snare many snappy morsels for his Scandal sheet. So-o-o-o things got hotly mixed up. There was a midnight bathing party for two ...and a fight ...and a wedding ...and how it all comes out makes THE PHILADELPHIA STORY the funniest film in years...which should cause you to roll in the aisles with laughter.

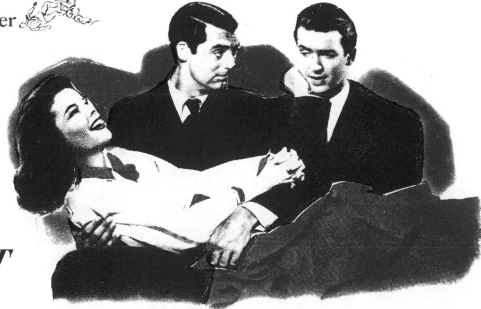

Cary GRANT

Katharine HEPBURN

James STEWART

THE PHILADELPHIA STORY

with RUTH HUSSEY

JOHN HOWARD · ROLAND YOUNG · JOHN HALLIDAY · MARY NASH · VIRGINIA WEIDLER
Screen Play by Donald Ogden Stewart · Based on the Play by Philip Barry
Produced by The Theatre Guild Inc. · Produced by JOSEPH L. MANKIEWICZ
Directed by GEORGE CUKOR · A Metro-Goldwyn-Mayer Picture

There's more about "PHILADELPHIA STORY" in the Lion's Roar Column on page 4

BEWITCHED
AND BEWILDERED!

"Eve sure knows her apples!"

"Girls, the best way to get a man is to get him bothered!"

Paramount Presents
BARBARA   HENRY
STANWYCK · FONDA
"THE LADY EVE"
Written and Directed by
PRESTON STURGES

PRESTON STURGES, Paramount's new writer-director genius, blends thrilling love and roaring laughter to give you the *vexiest* picture of the year.

with CHARLES COBURN · EUGENE PALLETTE
Martha O'Driscoll · William Demarest · Eric Blore
Screen Play Based on a Story by Monckton Hoffe

Ask your Theatre Manager when this Big Paramount Hit is coming—You'll want to see it twice!

—150—

On the screen in Technicolor for all America's millions... the play all America loves best!

All that red hair is in Technicolor now!

WARNER BROS. present Clarence Day's

LIFE WITH FATHER

starring WILLIAM **POWELL**

IRENE **DUNNE**

Welcome! The longest-run stage hit in history (8 straight years!) is a Warner Picture now! Heed the happy word of all who've already seen it and head for Warners' finest the first moment you can!

WB

with **ELIZABETH TAYLOR**

EDMUND GWENN · ZaSu PITTS
Screen Play by Donald Ogden Stewart
From Oscar Serlin's Stage Production
Music by Max Steiner

From the original play by
HOWARD LINDSAY & RUSSEL CROUSE

Directed by
MICHAEL CURTIZ

Produced by
ROBERT BUCKNER

The Power Behind The Throne

JANE FONDA   LILY TOMLIN   DOLLY PARTON

9 TO 5

AN IPC FILMS PRODUCTION OF A COLIN HIGGINS PICTURE

IN **NINE TO FIVE** DABNEY COLEMAN · ELIZABETH WILSON

and STERLING HAYDEN as The Chairman of the Board Produced by BRUCE GILBERT

Directed by COLIN HIGGINS Screenplay by COLIN HIGGINS and PATRICIA RESNICK

Story by PATRICIA RESNICK Music by CHARLES FOX

Starts Friday, December 19 at a theatre near you!

SHE WANTED BREAKFAST IN BED

...but she didn't want to eat alone!!!

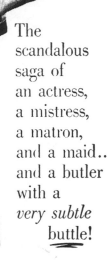

The scandalous saga of an actress, a mistress, a matron, and a maid.. and a butler with a *very subtle* buttle!

FROM BOUDOIR TO BASEMENT HE WAS THE MAN OF THE HOUSE!

JUNE ALLYSON DAVID NIVEN

MY MAN GODFREY

CinemaScope   in *Eastman* COLOR

co-starring **JESSIE ROYCE LANDIS**   **ROBERT KEITH**

EVA GABOR · **JAY ROBINSON**   **JEFF DONNELL** and **MARTHA HYER**

Universal International

Directed by **HENRY KOSTER**   Screenplay by EVERETT FREEMAN, PETER BERNEIS and WILLIAM BOWERS · Based on the screenplay by MORRIE RYSKIND and ERIC HATCH and on the novel by ERIC HATCH · Produced by ROSS HUNTER

A Universal International Picture

Only these two pigeons could dress up as woodpeckers...

and get framed for robbing a bank... and when these two cuckoos discover that prison life is for the birds they try to fly the coop before they go...

STIR CRAZY

School's out—it's Gable Day —a holiday in hilarity!

Physics: No two people can occupy the same space at the same time (but they can try!)

Chemistry: Compound of gin and vermouth is dangerous when shook!

Geometry: A curve is the nicest distance between two points!

Music: Latin rhythms have strange effects on blondes!

She calls herself "Little Instant Me!"

VistaVision®

SONGS:
"TEACHER'S PET"
"TEACHER'S PET MAMBO"
"THE GIRL WHO INVENTED ROCK AND ROLL"

Paramount presents

Clark Gable · Doris Day

in THE **PERLBERG -SEATON** PRODUCTION OF

Teacher's Pet

—ten years from today you'll still be talking about 58's Very Forward Look in Comedy!

co-starring

Gig Young · Mamie Van Doren

Produced by William Perlberg · Directed by George Seaton
Written by Fay and Michael Kanin · A Paramount Release

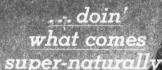

TIERNEY
with a taunting smile...
HARRISON
with a haunting kiss...

...doin' what comes super-naturally!

It's the man-woman affair like nothing on earth... from the best-seller that spread a sly smile across the face of America!

GENE TIERNEY · REX HARRISON · GEORGE SANDERS

The Ghost and Mrs. Muir

A 20th CENTURY-FOX ROMANCE!

with EDNA BEST · Vanessa Brown · Anna Lee · Robert Coote · Natalie Wood · Isobel Elsom · Victoria Horne

Directed by JOSEPH L. MANKIEWICZ · Produced by FRED KOHLMAR · Screen Play by Philip Dunne From the Novel by R. A. Dick

The Movie Ads